PAris by bike with velib'

PAris by bike with velib'

CHÊNE

Introduction

One, two, three, four, five …

It's already been six years since Vélib' – the handsome, streamlined bicycles with their little baskets – began accompanying Parisians in their daily lives. Whether to go and buy bread, visit a friend, head off to work, or an improvised picnic, there is always a Vélib' at hand! In fact, there are 1800 bike stations across Paris and its suburbs. To celebrate Vélib's anniversary, the Mayor of Paris, the *Vélib' & Moi* blog – a real platform for exchanges between users – and the Guides du Chêne present you seven rides along main streets and alleys, narrow cul-de-sacs and wide esplanades, capturing Paris's splendid buildings and its hidden treasures.

So, let's go! Perched on your saddle, explore a bit more of Paris: royal Paris with its grand museums, that attract increasing numbers of visitors from around the world, the working-class suburbs of the city, or still the green or trendy areas of Paris. (Re)discover the many facets of the capital, on your bike, at your leisure, while looking around you (but still keeping an eye on the traffic!). Using the flashcodes throughout the book, you can get real-time updates on the places you're visiting. Take advantage, too, of the *Vélib' & Moi* blog's top tips for gourmet bistros, sidewalk cafés, popular restaurants, and art galleries … All to recharge your batteries before pedalling off again! There's nothing simpler with 700 km (435 mi) of cycle lanes and 23,000 bicycles at your disposal. That's "Vélib'erty"! So, are you ready? Then on your bike!

The Vélib' & moi Blog

"My Parisian partner", that's how the *Vélib' & Moi* blog presents itself. Indeed, it's a real place of exchange, where members of the Vélib' community come to share tips and tricks, shopping ideas and travel suggestions. Bloggers are ready to dispense their advice and you will find all the information you need to make the most of your Vélib' excursions. You can also get a behind-the-scenes glimpse of the service operated by JCDecaux, via interviews and profiles of their operations, maintenance, and coordination leaders. Be sure to share your own tips, leave a comment, or ask a question. The blog allows you to respond to bloggers' messages, whatever the issue – from the latest news about the service, to recommendations for the capital's best restaurants or advice on cycling facilities.

AN INVITATION TO DISCOVER THE "REAL PARIS"

Composed of different sections (The Real Paris, Food, Nightlife, Culture and Shopping), the blog has something for everyone. Issues such as sustainable development, cycling and health, and the new face of Paris are addressed and you are welcome to join the debate. The *Vélib' & Moi* blog is useful for both Parisians and visitors, offering a view of Parisian life, a glimpse of little-known Paris, and everything you need to maxize the service. In addition to bringing Vélib' users together, the blog invites you to join the Vélib' community on other social networks, so that you can keep up to date on the Vélib' Twitter account (@ParisbyVelib), become a fan of the Vélib' Facebook page, try out new places on the Foursquare page, or rediscover Paris using our Instagram site.

Visit *blog.velib.paris.fr/en/*

Contents

9

How to Use Vélib'?

Above all, Vélib' is about having the freedom to go where you like, when you like; to cycle in the open air; and to enjoy all that the different areas of Paris have to offer. With 23,000 bicycles and nearly 1800 cycle stations in Paris and the 30 neighbouring municipalities, Vélib' offers a number of routes to explore the capital, its heritage, and its many attractions. From its 700 km (435 miles) of cycle paths and its 12 recommended routes, we have selected seven rides to (re)discover Paris. They are just waiting for you!

....

1. GO TO A VÉLIB' STATION

You will always be able to find a Vélib' station nearby as one is located approximately every 300 m (330 yds). Available 24/7, Vélib' is the perfect way to travel and make the most of your time in Paris. For locations of stations and available bikes, use the official Vélib smartphone app.

A map of the stations is also available on www.en.velib.paris.fr and on the Vélib terminal screens.

2. BUY YOUR VÉLIB' TICKET

The Vélib' stations are equipped with multilingual display terminals and a credit card payment system (Visa, Mastercard, JCB, American Express), where you can buy your Vélib' ticket. This ticket has a number that you will need to key in along with your personal code each time you use Vélib'. You can also buy a ticket up to 15 days in advance on www.en.velib.paris.fr, or by using the Vélib' app. Simple, fast and secure, online payment is possible with all smart cards. You will receive your ticket number and personal code via e-mail.

Velib'
MAIRIE DE PARIS

Scan this flashcode or visit:
For iPhones:
http://bit.ly/iphonevelib

For Androids:
http://bit.ly/androidvelib

For Windows Phones:
http://bit.ly/wpvelib

3. HOW MUCH DOES IT COST?

Vélib' offers 1-day (€1.70) and 7-days (€8) tickets. You can make as many trips as you like while your ticket is valid. A trip begins when you take a bike from the station and ends when you return it to the same or any other Vélib' station.

The first 30 minutes of each trip are free. Thereafter, the cost of each extra half hour is progressive: €1, €2 then €4 for each additional half hour. The trick is therefore to make short trips so as to return your bike before the end of the 30 free minutes. Vélib' also offers annual subscriptions from €19 on velib.paris.fr.

4. I'VE GOT MY TICKET. NOW HOW DO I TAKE MY VÉLIB'?

To get a Vélib', go to a terminal and type in your ticket number and personal code. You will be offered a bike among those available. Type in the number of the post your bike is locked on. To unlock your bike, press the button on top. Before taking your bike out, check its condition.

5. HOW DO I RETURN MY BIKE?

To return your bike, reinsert it in the bike post, and wait a few moments. The orange light will change to green, and you will hear two successive beeps. Only then can you be sure that your bike has been correctly returned and the rental time stopped.

6. WHAT DO I DO IF THERE ARE NO SPACES LEFT AT THE STATION?

Log in immediately at the terminal. The system will then offer you an additional 15 minutes to reach a nearby station, which you can see on the terminal's menu.

7. WHAT IS THE DEPOSIT FOR?

To use the service, you are required to pay a deposit of €150 (which is not cashed). You are responsible for your bike. The deposit is cashed by the service only in the event of non-compliance with the conditions of use or if the bike is not returned within 24 hours.

If you have a Carte Jeune, Visa Electron or Mastercard, your deposit may be temporarily debited by your bank to block this sum, which will be refunded to your account after the service's billing. You can check with your bank for more information about the terms of your credit or debit card. To travel safely, be attentive to what's going on around you and to other road users, and be careful of trucks' blind spots. Vélib' wishes you a wonderful time on the streets of Paris!

If you encounter problems, call us at 01 30 79 79 30, from a telephone or a terminal.

Paris in 7 Cycle Routes

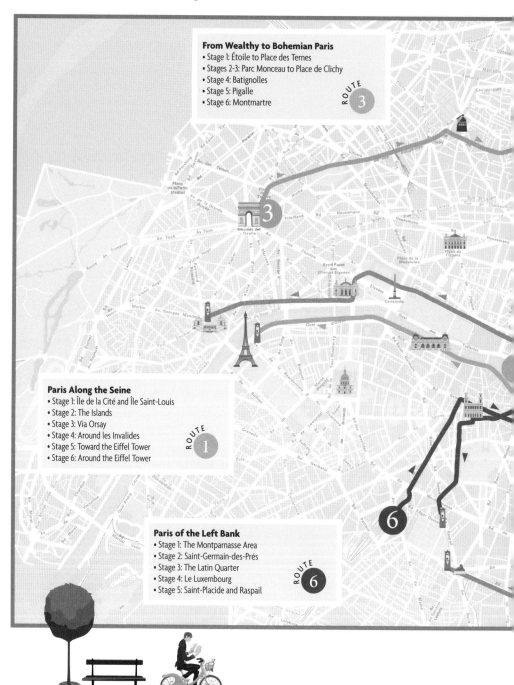

From Wealthy to Bohemian Paris
- Stage 1: Étoile to Place des Ternes
- Stages 2-3: Parc Monceau to Place de Clichy
- Stage 4: Batignolles
- Stage 5: Pigalle
- Stage 6: Montmartre

ROUTE 3

Paris Along the Seine
- Stage 1: Île de la Cité and Île Saint-Louis
- Stage 2: The Islands
- Stage 3: Via Orsay
- Stage 4: Around les Invalides
- Stage 5: Toward the Eiffel Tower
- Stage 6: Around the Eiffel Tower

ROUTE 1

Paris of the Left Bank
- Stage 1: The Montparnasse Area
- Stage 2: Saint-Germain-des-Prés
- Stage 3: The Latin Quarter
- Stage 4: Le Luxembourg
- Stage 5: Saint-Placide and Raspail

ROUTE 6

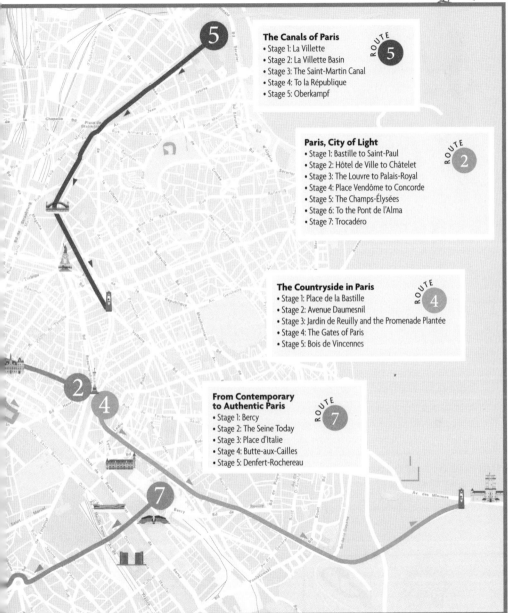

The Canals of Paris
- Stage 1: La Villette
- Stage 2: La Villette Basin
- Stage 3: The Saint-Martin Canal
- Stage 4: To la République
- Stage 5: Oberkampf

ROUTE **5**

Paris, City of Light
- Stage 1: Bastille to Saint-Paul
- Stage 2: Hôtel de Ville to Châtelet
- Stage 3: The Louvre to Palais-Royal
- Stage 4: Place Vendôme to Concorde
- Stage 5: The Champs-Élysées
- Stage 6: To the Pont de l'Alma
- Stage 7: Trocadéro

ROUTE **2**

The Countryside in Paris
- Stage 1: Place de la Bastille
- Stage 2: Avenue Daumesnil
- Stage 3: Jardin de Reuilly and the Promenade Plantée
- Stage 4: The Gates of Paris
- Stage 5: Bois de Vincennes

ROUTE **4**

From Contemporary to Authentic Paris
- Stage 1: Bercy
- Stage 2: The Seine Today
- Stage 3: Place d'Italie
- Stage 4: Butte-aux-Cailles
- Stage 5: Denfert-Rochereau

ROUTE **7**

Route 1

Paris Along the Seine

From Notre-Dame to the Eiffel Tower, via the Musée d'Orsay and the National Assembly, cycle along the Left Bank of the Seine and take in mythic and historic Paris, where some of the capital's finest buildings are to be found. Discover on your own pace picturesque views of the gardens on the riverbanks, next to which stand some of the world's most prestigious museums. And, as a plus, the route isn't difficult: it's a flat path!

STAGE 1 — ÎLE DE LA CITÉ AND ÎLE SAINT-LOUIS

✦ A Word From Vélib'

You will find four well-provisioned Vélib' stations on Île de la Cité. Cross the island from west to east to reach Île Saint-Louis via the bridge of the same name. Cycle back along the Quai d'Orléans and take the first bridge on your right, the Pont de la Tournelle, which will take you to the Left Bank.

Palais de Justice

Welcome to one of the chambers of the former Royal Palace, the seat of power (10th–14th centuries) until Charles V moved it to the Louvre. You can visit the palace and its numerous corridors, the Caesar Tower, the Silver Tower and best of all, the Bonbec Tower, the torture room where confessions were extorted from

suspects. It's still a place for confessions, but today they're obtained by much less barbarous means!

4 Bd. du Palais, 1ᵉʳ. 0892 683 000.
Access to hearings in the afternoon.
🅥 No. 01-01 (41 Quai de l'Horloge, 1ᵉʳ).

Conciergerie

The *concierge* was one of the principal members of the royal administration. Clovis established his "Conciergerie" here to maintain order and manage the police force and the prison.

2 Bd. du Palais, 1ᵉʳ. 01 53 40 60 80.
Open daily, 9:30am – 5pm. Admission fee.
🅥 No. 01-01 (41 Quai de l'Horloge, 1ᵉʳ).

ON THE ITINERARY

A tour of Paris's architectural heritage along the banks of the Seine, leaving from Île de la Cité and cycling via Île Saint-Louis, Saint-Germain-des-Prés, the Musée d'Orsay, and the Quai Branly to the Eiffel Tower.

Departure Point:
Île de la Cité (No. 01-01 – 41, Quai de l'Horloge, 4ᵉ)

Arrival Point:
Champs-de-Mars, (No. 007-23 – Quai Branly, 7ᵉ)

Sainte-Chapelle

This edifice at the heart of the Palais de la Cité, built from 1242 to 1248 at the instigation of Saint Louis to house the relics of Christ, is a magnificent example of the Rayonnant period of Gothic architecture. In the upper chapel, 15 stained-glass windows relate 1113 scenes from the Old Testament; the lower chapel houses an Annunciation scene, the oldest wall painting in Paris.

8 Bd. du Palais, 1ᵉʳ. 01 53 40 60 80.
www.sainte-chapelle.monuments-nationaux.fr
Open daily, 9:30am–6pm. Admission fee.
🅥 No. 04-02 (Pl. Louis-Lépine, 4ᵉ)

Pont des Arts

Pont-Neuf

The oldest bridge in Paris, despite its name, is located at the eastern tip of Île de la Cité. Commissioned by Henri IV, it was built during the late 16th and early 17th centuries. Its uniqueness lies in the fact that it was the first bridge to be devoid of houses, and to have pavements allowing Parisians to admire the Seine. A revolution! Its architecture with half-moon bastions was designed by Desilles and Androuet du Cerceau. Climb up its steps to see the island's fortifications and reach the Square du Vert-Galant.

🅥 No. 01-01 (41 Quai de l'Horloge, 1ᵉʳ).

Square du Vert-Galant

The Vert-Galant (Green Gallant) was Henri IV, who made no pretense about his numerous love affairs. This square, with a statue of him made in 1834, reminds one of this character traits. It's a romantic spot planted with different species of trees (Prunus, maples, willows), and it's perfect for a picnic by the river, with a splendid view of the Pont Neuf, the Louvre, and the Seine. On a nice day, go to the tip of the island, under the weeping willow, to see the sun set over the Seine.

🅥 No. 01-01 (41 Quai de l'Horloge, 1ᵉʳ).

STAGE 6

- Eiffel Tower
- Champ-de-Mars
- Pont de Bir-Hakeim
- Île aux Cygnes

- Le Suffren
- Erawan
- Le Beaujolais
- Eiffel Club
- Café Primerose
- Thé aux trois Cerises

ALMA MARCEAU

08-45

PT DE L'ALMA

JARDIN FLOTTANT

PT DES INVALIDES

5

PONT DE L'ALMA

QUAI D'ORSAY

ÉGLISE AMÉRICAINE

07-23

QUAI BRANLY

MUSÉE DU QUAI BRANLY

07-22

RUE DE L'UNIVERSITÉ

07-16

BD DE LA TOUR-MAUBOURG

6

La Seine

PT D'IENA

AV. BOSQUET

RUE ST-DOMINIQUE

TOUR EIFFEL

AV. DE LA BOURDONNAIS

07-24

07-21

RUE CLERC

RUE DE GRENELLE

LA TOUR MAUBOURG

ES DES

07-25

07-103

07-17

HÔ IN\

CHAMP DE MARS TOUR EIFFEL

07-19

PARC DU CHAMP-DE-MARS

ÉCOLE MILITAIRE

15-71

AV. TOURVILLE

BIR-HAKEIM

RUE DE LA FÉDÉRATION

AV. DE SUFFREN

15-26

AV. DE LA MOTTE PICQUET

904

15-105

15-25

15-24

DUPLEIX

15-106

15-23

LA MOTTE PICQUET GRENELLE

RUE DE BIR-HAKEIM

- Floating Gardens
- Musée du Quai Branly
- Pont de l'Alma
- Place de l'Alma

- Café de Mars
- Les Ombres
- Vin sur Vin
- Pottoka
- Le Bardelo
- Comptoirs Bourdonnais
- Chattanooga
- Les Deux Abeilles

STAGE 5

PLACE DE LA CONCORDE

RUE DE RIVOLI

TUILERIES Ⓜ

PT DE LA CONCORDE

QUAI DES TUILERIES

4

BERGES LA DE SEINE

QUAI ANATOLE-FRANCE

ASSEMBLÉE NATIONALE

ASSEMBLÉE NATIONALE Ⓜ

MUSÉE D'ORSAY

MUSÉE D'ORSAY

RUE DE L'UNIVERSITÉ

PALAIS DE LA LÉGION D'HONNEUR

07-11 07-09
Ⓥ   Ⓥ

BD ST-GERMAIN

RUE ST-DOMINIQUE

07-08 07-07
Ⓥ   Ⓥ

3

PT ROYAL

QUAI DU LOUVRE

PALAIS ROYAL MUSÉE DU LOUVRE

· École Nationale Supérieure des Beaux-Arts
· Musée d'Orsay
· Large Stairway on the Banks of the Seine
· Palais de la Légion d'honneur

🍸 · L'Hôtel
🍽 · L'Affable
· Ze Kitchen Gallerie
· Yen
· Concorde Atlantique
🛍 · Le Grand Comptoir My Store
· Ladurée

STAGE **3**

RUE DE GRENELLE

SOLFÉRINO Ⓜ

QUAI VOLTAIRE

RUE DU BAC

RUE DE LILLE

07-06 Ⓥ

QUAI MALAQUAIS

PT DU CARROUSEL

PT DES ARTS

SQ. VERT

QUAI DE CONTI

Ⓥ 07-15

🍴🍽

RUE DE L'UNIVERSITÉ

RUE DES SAINTS-PÈRES

ÉCOLE DES BEAUX-ARTS

RUE BONAPARTE

06-01 Ⓥ

Ⓜ VARENNE

RUE DU BAC Ⓜ

BD ST-GERMAIN

06-21

06-13 Ⓥ   06-14

· Pont de la Concorde
· Assemblée Nationale
· Esplanade des Invalides
· Hôtel des Invalides

🥂 · Le Gatsby
· Il Vino
· Chez l'Ami Jean
· L'Éclair
· La culée du pont Alexandre-III
· Michel Chaudun
· La Boulangerie Poujauran

STAGE **4**

BD RASPAIL

RUE DU BAC

ST-GERMAIN DES PRÉS Ⓜ

06-15 Ⓥ

MABILLON

R. DU FOUR

R. MABILLON Ⓜ

ODÉON Ⓜ

RUE DE RENNES

RUE DE SÈVRES

RUE DE VAUGIRARD

· Palais de Justice
· Conciergerie
· Sainte-Chapelle
· Pont-Neuf
· Square Vert-Galant
· Place Dauphine
· Pont des Arts

• La Réserve de Quasimodo
• Les Fous de l'île
• Isami
• Théâtre de l'île Saint-Louis
  Paul-Rey
• 78ISL
• Berthillon

STAGE 1

· Île de la Cité
· Notre-Dame
· Archeological Crypt in Front
  of Notre-Dame
· Île Saint-Louis
· Institut du Monde Arabe
· Jardin Tino-Rossi

• 43 Up the Roof
• Prescription Cocktail Club
• Le Caveau des Oubliettes
• Shakespeare & Company
• Maison Kayser

STAGE 2

CHÂTELET
LES HALLES

PALAIS R
MUSÉE DU

RER

LOUVRE
RIVOLI

RUE DE RIVOLI

01-101
PONT NEUF

QUAI DE LA MÉGISSERIE

CHÂTELET

SQ. VERT-GALANT

1

PT NEUF

01-01

QUAI DE GESVRES

HÔTEL
DE VILLE

QUAI DE CONTI

CONCIÈRGERIE

PT AU-
CHANGE

PALAIS DE JUSTICE

ÎLE DE LA CITÉ

QUAI D'ARCOLE

QUAI DE L'HÔTEL-DE-VILLE

STE CHAPELLE

04-02

ST-PAUL

CITÉ

QUAI DES ORFÈVRES

06-14

QUAI DES GDS-AUGUSTINS

04-01

06-15

NOTRE-DAME

04-03

PONT MARIE

06-20

06-16

ST-MICHEL

05-33

RUE ST-LOUIS-EN-L'ILE

ODÉON

05-01

R DU PETIT-PONT

QUAI DE MONTEBELLO

05-09

R DES 2 PONTS

ÎLE SAINT-LOUIS

CLUNY
LA SORBONNE

05-08

PT DE SULLY

05-107

BD ST-MICHEL

BD ST-GERMAIN

QUAI DE LA TOURNELLE

R DE LA
TOURNELLE

RUE ST-JACQUES

MAUBERT
MUTUALITÉ

05-19

05-20

RUE DES ÉCOLES

JARDIN
TINO-ROSSI

R DES FOSSÉS-ST-BERNARD

INSTITUT DU
MONDE ARABE

Place Dauphine

In the past there were two islets; they were joined in the 16th century by this elegant square dedicated to the Dauphin, Louis XIII. (French singer Jacques Dutronc used to sing *"Je suis le dauphin de la place Dauphine".*) Thirty-two brick, stone, and slate houses added to the grandeur of this triangular-shaped square, two examples of which can still be admired at the tip of the island. After much architectural restructuring – clearings and redevelopments – the square is today shaded by chestnut trees and frequented by romantic tourists.

🅥 No. 01-01 (41 Quai de l'Horloge, 1er).

Pont des Arts

Linking the two banks of the Seine, opposite the French Institute, stands the Pont des Arts – a footbridge and the first metal bridge in Paris, constructed in 1801. Rebuilt in 1981, it lost two arches and now has only seven. Today it has a new function: lovers from all over the world come here to lock padlocks, sealing their love, onto the bridge's metal railings. In the evenings, Parisians flock here *en masse* to have a picnic in a festive atmosphere.

Between Quai du Louvre (1er) and Quai Malaquais (6e).
🅥 No. 06-01 (5 Quai Malaquais, 6e).

Taking a Break

LA RÉSERVE DE QUASIMODO
Tucked away in an alley in the shadow of Notre-Dame, this wine bar is a perfect place to unwind at the end of the day. Its wine cellar offers a selection of wines in the comfortable ambience of an old-world inn. Spirit lovers are not forgotten either with its fine collection of traditional Armagnac and pastis.
🍸 4 Rue Colombe, Paris 4e. 01 46 34 67 67.
Open Tue–Sun, noon–10pm.
🅥 No. 04-01 (10 Rue d'Arcole, 4e).

LES FOUS DE L'ÎLE
People come to this traditional bistro on Île Saint-Louis to enjoy a tartare, Berthillon ice cream, or simply to have a drink. The set menus are reasonably priced for the area (starter, main course, and dessert for €27 in the evening).
🍽 33 Rue des Deux-Ponts, 4e. 01 43 25 76 67.
www.lesfousdelile.com – Open daily, noon–11pm.
🅥 No. 04-03 (1 Quai aux Fleurs, 4e).

THÉÂTRE DE L'ÎLE SAINT-LOUIS PAUL REY
The smallest theatre in Paris is popular for its intimate space and character. From classical music to theatre, poetry to pop, here, anything goes! Come and enjoy piano recitals at 6:30pm and other performances at 9pm.
🎭 39 Quai d'Anjou, 4e. 01 46 33 48 65.
www.theatre-ilesaintlouis.com
🅥 No. 04-03 (1 Quai aux Fleurs, 4e).

ISAMI
This Japanese restaurant is considered by many Parisians to be the place to eat raw fish in the capital. The list of sakes is also of top quality.
🍽 4 Quai d'Orléans, 4e. 01 40 46 06 97. Closed Mon.
🅥 No. 04-03 (1 Quai aux Fleurs, 4e).

78ISL
This multi-brand shop sells fashion that's at the forefront of the latest trends. Discover labels such as Vero Moda, Suncoo Paris, LTB Jeans, and Blend, as well as a fine selection of leather goods (€20 for a clutch, €85 for a handbag).
🛍 78 Rue Saint-Louis-en-l'Île, 4e. 01 40 46 06 36.
www.78isl.com – Open daily, 10:30am–7:30pm.
🅥 No. 04-03 (1 Quai aux Fleurs, 4e).

BERTHILLON
At this ice-cream parlour – the most famous one in Paris – you'll be unable to resist the raspberry and chocolate sorbets, and the candied chestnut ice cream.
🍦 31 Rue Saint-Louis-en-l'Île, 4e. 01 43 54 31 61.
www.berthillon.fr – Open Wed–Sun, 10am–8pm.
🅥 No. 04-03 (1 Quai aux Fleurs, 4e).

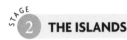
⭐ **A Word From Vélib'** ·····················

Use the bike lane on the upper quay, instead of the more cobbled one below. Ride along next to the booksellers, enjoying the view of the islands from the centre of Paris, until you reach the Musée d'Orsay. It's easy – just keep going straight ahead!

Île de la Cité

This is without doubt Paris's most famous island. The city's historic birthplace and today a tourist mecca, it was formerly known as Lutetia until Clovis decided to make it his capital. It was then developed around a maze of cobbled streets and crooked houses, which were demolished by Napoleon III, making space for Haussmann's architecture.

🅥 No. 01-01 (41 Quai de l'Horloge, 1er).

Notre-Dame

Cycling on the Île de la Cité, you can't miss this impressive jewel in the crown of Medieval art (12th–14th centuries), which recently celebrated its 850th anniversary. From the forecourt of the cathedral, admire the Portal of the Last Judgement, showing Hell on the left of Christ and Paradise on the right. Walk around the left of the building to see the superb restoration (2011) of the little red door, that gives access to the cloister). Guided tours are free and the view from the top of the tower is magnificent.

6 Pl. du Parvis-Notre-Dame, place Jean-Paul-II, 4e. 01 42 34 56 10. www.notredamedeparis.fr
Open daily, 8am–6:45pm
🅥 No. 04-01 (10 Rue d'Arcole, 4e).

Notre-Dame Cathedral

Archeological Crypt in front of Notre-Dame

In this amazing place, where you would never imagine finding so many archeological remains, you can trace more than 2000 years of the city's history. Paris was built on the site of the Gallo-Roman city of Lutetia, with its baths and shipbuilding around Sequana (the ancestor of the Seine). The crypt has a large number of ruins, including stones from an ancient fourth-century wall that once enclosed the city. This is also the place to admire the genius of Baron Haussmann with his famous sewers.

7 Pl. du Parvis-Notre-Dame, 4e. 01 55 42 50 10. www.crypte.paris.fr – Open Tue–Sun, 10am–6pm. Closed public holidays. Admission fee.
🅥 No. 04-01 (10 Rue d'Arcole, 4e).

Île Saint-Louis

Want to escape the crowds of tourists? Then get back on your Vélib', and cross the Seine on the Pont Saint-Louis to get to Île Saint-Louis. Quieter than the neighbouring Île de la Cité, it is no less charming. A stroll around its streets will allow you to appreciate the Baroque Saint-Louis-en-l'Île church, as well as the architecture of the old mansions with their wrought-iron balconies and elegant stone facades. At one time, Baudelaire and Balzac used to meet here in private clubs. The sign "Au Franc Pinot", which is still visible on the Quai de Bourbon, is a reminder of the wild nightlife of this former cabaret.

Don't go looking for a Vélib' station on this island; there isn't one, just as there isn't a metro station!

The city's riverbanks on a sunny day

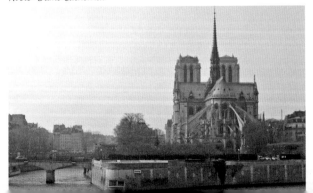

Institut du Monde Arabe

This unusual place, entirely devoted to the culture of the Arab world, with a museum and temporary exhibitions, is housed in a building designed by Jean Nouvel. Leave your bike at the station opposite to admire the facade pierced with 240 *mashrabiya* that are kept open according to the amount of sunlight. In the library inside, a spiral tower of books is reminiscent of the architecture of minarets. A café, bookstore, restaurant and terrace complete the experience for the visitor.

1 Rue des Fossés-Saint-Bernard, 5ᵉ. 01 40 51 38 38.
www.imarabe.com – Open daily, 10am–7pm.
🚲 No. 05-20 (3 Rue des Fossés-Saint-Bernard, 5ᵉ).

Jardin Tino-Rossi

This is the perfect place to add something special to a romantic walk or a Sunday picnic. With its magnificent view of Notre-Dame, the comings and goings of barges on the river, and its sculptures by Brancusi, César and Zadkine, the square provides couples who love to dance with a unique place to practise facing the Seine. So have a picnic or a drink on the terraces before you hit the dance floor: salsa, tango, rock … there's something for everyone!

Quai Saint-Bernard, 5ᵉ.
🚲 No. 05-20 (3 Rue des Fossés-Saint-Bernard, 5ᵉ).

Taking a Break

43 UP THE ROOF

This is an address that Parisians guard jealously. Situated on the roof of the Holiday Inn Paris Notre-Dame, the bar offers a panoramic view of Paris that takes your breath away! And you can enjoy delicious cocktails here.
🍸 4 Rue Danton, 6ᵉ. Res. required. 01 80 69 00 60.

Open Tue–Sat, 4pm–midnight.
🚲 No. 06-20 (2 Rue Danton, 6ᵉ).

SHAKESPEARE AND COMPANY

A bookstore that never ceases to surprise, with new, second-hand, and rare books. The owner is a legend as well!
📖 37 Rue de la Bûcherie, 5ᵉ. 01 43 25 40 93
www.shakespeareandcompany.com – Open daily, 10am–11pm.
🚲 No. 05-09 (6 Rue du Fouarre, 5ᵉ).

The Shakespeare and Company bookstore

PRESCRIPTION COCKTAIL CLUB

In this trendy bar in Saint-Germain you can sip a cocktail in the company of TV reporters and models awaiting Fashion Week. Its atmosphere evokes the prohibition era. A word of advice – get here early on the weekend!
🍸 23 Rue Mazarine, 6ᵉ. 01 46 34 67 73.
www.prescriptioncocktailclub.com. Open daily, 6pm–1am.
🚲 No. 06-13 (1 Rue Jacques-Callot, 6ᵉ).

MAISON KAYSER

What an incredible variety of breads: saucisson and red wine, rose, white chocolate …!
The plain, chocolate, and pistachio financiers, *moelleux*, and *fondants* also make Parisians' mouths water.
🥖 8 Rue Monge, Paris 5ᵉ. 01 44 07 01 42.
www.maison-kayser.com – Open Wed–Mon, 6:45am–8:30pm.
🚲 No. 05-18 (20 Rue Monge, 5ᵉ).

CAVEAU DES OUBLIETTES

This jazz mecca showcases a different style of music every night. You can listen to up-and-coming funk and jazz artists here, as well as ska, punk, and reggae. Entrance is free but the drinks are a bit expensive.
🎷 52 Rue Galande, 5ᵉ. 01 46 34 23 09.
www.caveaudesoubliettes.fr – Open daily, 5pm–4am.
🚲 No. 05-09 (6 Rue du Fouarre, 5ᵉ).

⭐ A Word From Vélib'

When you arrive at the Musée d'Orsay, you can either continue your ride along the upper quay to enjoy the buildings of the Left Bank, or cycle along the recently redeveloped lower banks of the Seine. Our choice would be the latter: a wonderful 2.5 km (1.5 mi) ride.

École Nationale Supérieure des Beaux-Arts

It was Queen Margot who assembled the first art collections in the Chapelle des Louanges, at the heart of the Augustinian convent. Three centuries later, the Beaux Arts studio was working at full capacity on the famous posters of May 1968. The successor of the Royal Academy of Painting and Sculptures founded by Louis XIV, it became the École Nationale des Beaux-Arts in 1816. Don't miss the recently restored glass-roofed courtyard of the Palais des Études.

14 Rue Bonaparte, 6ᵉ. 01 47 03 50 00
Ⓥ No. 06-21 (17 Rue des Beaux-Arts, 6ᵉ).

Musée d'Orsay

One of the largest museums in France, the Musée d'Orsay houses a splendid collection of Impressionist paintings, including *Le Déjeuner sur l'herbe* and *Olympia*, as well as Courbet's famous *Origine du monde*. The metal-and-glass surroundings also contain Western paintings and sculptures from 1848 to 1914. The place is worth seeing for its architecture, too. A former palace – the Court of Audit was based here for a time – then a train station (Paris-Orléans), it was restored between 1983 and 1986, making it into a perfect place in which to display art of the late 19th and early 20th centuries.

62 Rue de Lille, 7ᵉ. 01 40 49 48 14. www.musee-orsay.fr
Open Tue–Sun, 9:30am–6pm (Thu 9:45). Admission fee.
Ⓥ No. 07-07 (62 Rue de Lille, 7ᵉ).

Large Stairway on the Banks of the Seine

On the Quai Anatole-France, this flight of steps links the upper quay, where the Musée d'Orsay is situated, to the newly refurbished banks of the Seine. Several times a year, this large stairway becomes a venue that hosts, among other events, open-air screenings. Since spring 2013, the 2.4 km (1.5 mi) of the Left Bank have been reserved for pedestrians and cyclists (ride carefully!) Don't miss the bank's leisure and culture areas, which have been classed by UNESCO as a World Heritage Site.

www.bergesdeseine.paris.fr
Ⓥ No. 07-07 (62 Rue de Lille, 7ᵉ).

Palais de la Légion d'honneur

Discover the medals that the French nation has awarded its heroes, from the time of the Crusades to the present day. Built in 1782 at the request of Prince Frederick of Salm-Kyrbourg, the palace today houses the Musée National de la Légion d'Honneur et des Ordres de Chevalerie. Its contemporary gallery is devoted to the First World War.

2 Rue de la Légion-d'Honneur, 7ᵉ. 01 40 62 84 25.
www.musee-legiondhonneur.fr – Open Wed–Sun, 1–6pm.
Ⓥ No. 07-07 (62 Rue de Lille, 7ᵉ).

 ALSO WORTH SEEING ON THE WAY

THE VIEW FROM THE PONT DU CARROUSEL ★ ★ ★

HÔTEL DE BEAUHARNAIS ★

Calendar of Events
Exhibitions at the Musée d'Orsay
Scan this flashcode or visit
http://blog.velib.paris.fr/
en/?s=museequaiorsayEN

Taking a Break

L'HÔTEL

Install yourself comfortably in a velvet armchair in this former haunt of Oscar Wilde, Johnny Depp and Vanessa Paradis, and succumb to the temptation of a violet and champagne cocktail. Behind the red drapes, under the archway, you will find a swimming pool, which you can rent out for an hour or a day.

🍸 13 Rue des Beaux-Arts, 6ᵉ. 01 44 41 99 00. www.l-hotel.com

🚇 No. 06-21 (17 Rue des Beaux-Arts, 6ᵉ).

LADURÉE

An absolute must after a good bike ride, this *salon de thé* is famous for its colourful macarons, which will delight the taste buds of every gourmet. Heavenly pastries and fine food are on the menu in a charming setting. You will be equally captivated by its enchanting decor, painted walls, and very elegant furniture.

🍰 21 Rue Bonaparte, 6ᵉ. 01 44 07 64 87. www.laduree.fr
Open Mon–Fri, 8:30am–7:30pm; Sat, 8:30am–8:30pm; Sun and public holidays, 10:30am–7:30pm.

🚇 No. 06-02 (1 Rue Saint-Benoît, 6ᵉ).

L'AFFABLE

This little restaurant is entirely typical of the way that bistros have developed in the capital. Sit down on a red banquette in this chic bistro and enjoy some fine food, all of which is made on the premises using fresh produce. The set lunch menus are very good value for money.

🍽 10 Rue Saint-Simon, 7ᵉ. 01 42 22 01 60. www.laffable.fr – Closed Mon.

🚇 No. 07-05 (2 Bd. Raspail, 7ᵉ).

ZE KITCHEN GALLERIE

Here there are works of contemporary art on the walls, as well as on the plates. This is one of the bastions of Parisian fusion cuisine. It's not cheap, but you will get what you pay for. The set menu costs €70.

🍽 4 Rue des Grands-Augustins, 6ᵉ. 01 44 32 00 32. www.zekitchengalerie.fr – Closed Sun.

🚇 No. 06-14 (7 Rue du Pont-de-Lodi, 6ᵉ).

YEN

This is sort of the "celebrity" Japanese restaurant of the Left Bank, famous for its *soba*, Japanese noodles made from buckwheat flour, which you can enjoy with vegetable tempura or simmered pork. Treat your palate to an exotic holiday!

🍽 22 Rue Saint-Benoît, 6ᵉ. 01 45 44 11 18. Closed Sun.

🚇 No. 06-02 (1 Rue Saint-Benoît, 6ᵉ).

CONCORDE ATLANTIQUE

This three-level, 450m² (4844ft²) boat will host you for an evening of entertainment at the foot of the National Assembly and the Musée d'Orsay. It's one of the most sought-after venues by event planners for its beautiful terrace and two rooms. Prepare yourself for a pleasant stationary voyage at the whim of the Seine's waves.

🚢 23 Quai Anatole-France, 7ᵉ. 01 47 05 71 03. www.bateauconcordeatlantique.com

🚇 No. 07-09 (119 Rue de Lille, 7ᵉ).

LE GRAND COMPTOIR MY STORE

Clothing, fashion, interior decorations, perfume… you can find something and something for everyone in this shop, adults or children like! The product selection criteria are elegance, quality and price, and the wide range encourages eclecticism and colours. It's the perfect place to find an original gift.

🛍 116 Rue du Bac, 7ᵉ. 01 40 49 00 95.
Open Mon noon–7pm, Tue–Sat 10:30am–7pm.

🚇 No. 07-04 (28 Bd. Raspail, 7ᵉ).

23

Calendar of Events

Events on the banks of the Seine
Scan this flashcode or visit
http://blog.velib.paris.fr/en/
?s=bergesdeseineEN

🌸 A Word From Vélib' ·····················

The Eiffel Tower is peaking out! You're not far from your destination! Continue along the banks of the Seine or the Quai d'Orsay, while admiring the Right Bank, the National Assembly and the Hôtel des Invalides.

Pont de la Concorde

This bridge has spanned the Seine, from the Place de la Concorde to the Quai d'Orsay since 1775, which is very close to the time of the French Revolution. This meant that its architect was able to reuse stones for the structure from the Bastille, which had just fallen. Napoleon I erected the statues of generals killed in battle. The arched bridge was doubled in width in the early 20th century.

🅥 No. 07-09 (119 Rue de Lille, 7ᵉ).

Assemblée Nationale

Are you passionate about history and politics? The Bourbon Palace, which houses the National Assembly, is an unmissable place, where the public can attend parliamentary debates. Visit the palace's different rooms, from the Salle des Pas-Perdus, whose ceilings are the work of painter Horace Vernet, to the Salle des Séances, which gathers the 577 members of the National Assembly, via the splendid library with its 700,000 volumes.

126 Rue de l'Université and 33 Quai d'Orsay, Paris 7ᵉ. 01 40 63 60 00. www.assemblee-nationale.fr
🅥 No. 07-09 (119 Rue de Lille, 7ᵉ).

Esplanade des Invalides

On the north side of the Hôtel des Invalides, people laze around on the huge lawn that separates the place from the Quai d'Orsay. Since it was designed in the 18th century by Robert de Cotte, this esplanade has hosted many demonstrations – during the Revolution or to celebrate military triumphs at the end of various wars. Hundreds of different sports are played here as soon as spring arrives.

🅥 No. 07-10 (3 Rue de Constantine, 7ᵉ).

Hôtel des Invalides

The dome of Les Invalides was re-covered with 500,000 sheets of gold leaf during its restoration for the bicentenary of the French Revolution. Its church houses Napoleon's tomb. You can also visit the Église Saint-Louis des Invalides as well as the Musée des Plans-Reliefs, the Musée de l'Ordre de la Libération and the Musée de l'Armée, the latter of which is dedicated to the history of the French army. The Hôtel des Invalides was built at the instigation of Louis XIV for his disabled soldiers. It now houses a state-of-the-art surgical hospital.

Place Vauban, 7ᵉ. 01 44 42 38 77.
www.musee-armee.fr
🅥 No. 07-17 (1 Av. de la Motte-Picquet, 7ᵉ).

ALSO WORTH SEEING ON THE WAY

HÔTEL DE BRIENNE ★
THE AMERICAN CHURCH ★ ★

Heading toward the lawns of Les Invalides

Taking a Break

LE GATSBY

This trendy bar/restaurant on the Avenue Bosquet has given the area a new lease on life. In its cosy-chic ambience with 1920s-style wood panelling, you can enjoy tasty cocktails created by the bartenders. Jazz concerts are organized regularly in the vaulted basement to remain faithful to the spirit of the era.

64 Av. Bosquet, 7ᵉ. 01 45 55 02 79.
open Mon–Fri, noon-3pm and 7pm–2am.
No. 07-19 (85 Av. Bosquet, 7ᵉ).

CHEZ L'AMI JEAN

You're headed for Basque Country! Ami Jean is one of the finest examples of the capital's gastro-bistro trend. Backed by a great team, chef Stéphane Jego offers exceptional food with recipes that change daily. Creativity and quality are his hallmarks, and he takes pride in having a special relationship with his numerous suppliers. A word of advice: bring a full wallet!

27 Rue Malar, 7ᵉ. 01 47 05 86 89.
www.lamijean.fr – Open noon–2pm and 7pm–midnight.
No. 07-21 (37 Av. Bosquet, 7ᵉ).

BOULANGERIE POUJAURAN

The greatest names in French cuisine swear by the bread from this bakery to accompany their dishes. This bakery legend also makes the best *cannelés* in Paris and incredibly creamy *chaussons aux amandes*, which are spiced up with a touch of chocolate. Yum-yum!

20 Rue Jean-Nicot, 7ᵉ. 01 43 17 35 20.
Open Tue–Sat, 9:30am–8:30pm.
No. 07-16 (13 Rue Surcouf, 7ᵉ).

L'Éclair

IL VINO

Wine lovers will be in paradise here! Il Vino is the latest creation of the Best Sommelier of the World, and offers more than 1500 different wines from outstanding vineyards. Although most people come here above all for the wine, Enrico Bernardo also serves small, refined dishes to accompany them.

13 Bd. de la Tour-Maubourg, 7ᵉ. 01 44 11 72 00.
www.enricobernado.com – Open daily, noon–midnight.
No. 07-16 (13 Rue Surcouf, 7ᵉ).

MICHEL CHAUDUN

Welcome to chocolate lovers' heaven! Michel Chaudun, a passionate artist, has won many awards for his creations. He was responsible for the invention of cocoa nib-flecked chocolate in 1993, but his ganache cubes are also very popular. According to French TV celebrity and food critic, Jean-Pierre Coffe, Michel Chaudun's chocolates are fresh, sophisticated, original, and close to perfection.

149 Rue de l'Université, 7ᵉ. 01 47 53 74 40.
Open Mon, 9:30am–6pm; Tue–Sat, 9:15am–7pm.
No. 07-16 (13 Rue Surcouf, 7ᵉ).

L'ÉCLAIR

Sit back and enjoy unusual cocktails in a totally recycled vintage world that stands out from the posh places in the neighbourhood. In addition to the original decor, the café/bar serves up cocktails with amazing names and flavours. To accompany them, plates of cold meats and cheese will hit the spot if you're feeling peckish.

32 Rue Cler, 7ᵉ. 01 44 18 09 04. Open daily, 7am–2am.
No. 07-20 (3 Rue du Champs-de-Mars, 7ᵉ).

CULÉE DU PONT ALEXANDRE-III

Under the arches of the Pont Alexandre-III, this restaurant hosts artistic and cultural events that change throughout the day and year. Leisure activities and entertainment are also available on a new barge moored by the quai.

Esplanade des Invalides, 7ᵉ.
No. 07-10 (3 Rue de Constantine, 7ᵉ).

25

⭐ **A Word From Vélib'** • • • • • • • • • • • • • • • •

The Eiffel Tower has disappeared behind the Haussmann buildings, but don't worry, you're heading in the right direction! Continue along the Quai Branly; the *Dame de Fer* (Iron Lady) awaits you at the end of the bike path.

also a lovely restaurant on the roof and a well-stocked bookstore.

37 Quai Branly, 7ᵉ. 01 56 61 70 00. www.quaibranly.fr Open Tue–Sun, 11am–7pm. Admission fee.
ⓥ No. 07-23 (Quai Branly, 7ᵉ).

Floating Gardens

Moored to the banks of the Seine, this floating garden composed of five islands offers a novel place for a stroll. The central islands and its terraces invite you to relax at the water's edge. Île Prairie has a sort of giant hammock, a fun rope structure on which you can lie down above the tall grasses and that can accommodate up to 140 people – the perfect spot for the Nuit des étoiles (the summertime astronomical show)! On Île aux Oiseaux, the visitors keep quiet and make themselves inconspicuous in an open-air aviary. Here you can see birds that have come here freely to nest in the trees and shrubs.

Port du Gros-Caillou, 7ᵉ. ⓥ No. 07-22 (3 Av. Bosquet, 7ᵉ).

Musée du Quai Branly

Step into the museum's Japanese garden and you will be transported to the heart of Panama and even further away! In this green setting, boxes of colour assemble the different continents, reflecting the cultures of Asia, Africa, the Americas, and Oceania. This is one of Jean Nouvel's latest Parisian buildings, with a green wall by Patrick Blanc and a large picture window overlooking the quay. Behind the garden you will find the museum, with meandering ramps leading to different tribal art exhibitions. There's

Pont de l'Alma

The Pont de l'Alma has a slightly odd distinction: when the water level of the Seine reaches the Zouave's thighs, the Seine is no longer navigable. The original stone bridge, built by Napoleon III in 1854, to commemorate the Battle of Alma in the Crimean War, was adorned with four statues of soldiers (the statue of the Zouave is the only one left), representing the four regiments. Today's bridge, replaced in 1974, is made entirely of metal and is wider, to facilitate traffic flow.

ⓥ No. 07-22 (3 Av. Bosquet, 7ᵉ).

Place de l'Alma

Right by the Pont de l'Alma stands a replica of the flame of the Statue of Liberty, which was given to France by the Herald Tribune, in memory of the same gift given by France to the United States a few decades before. Today the square preserves the memory of another figure, Princess Diana, who died following her accident beneath the Pont de l'Alma in 1997. Since the princess's death, the flame has become a sort of Diana memorial, to which many people come every day to pay their respects.

ⓥ No. 07-22 (3 Av. Bosquet, 7ᵉ) or 08-45 (3 Av. Montaigne, 8ᵉ).

The very handy bike path in front of the museum

The Zouave

26

Taking a Break

CAFÉ DE MARS
This unpretentious bistro behind the Eiffel Tower serves simple but sophisticated food in a 1920s decor, and has a modest, but good wine list on hand.

11 Rue Augereau, 7ᵉ. 01 45 50 10 90.
Open Mon–Fri 11am–3pm, Sat 7pm–1am, Sun 11am–4pm.
www.cafedemars.com
No. 07-24 (43 Av. Rapp, 7ᵉ).

LES OMBRES
After all your hard work, it's time to relax! Go to the Quai Branly Museum to have a bite to eat in this world-fusion gourmet restaurant, which is as modern as the museum itself. The roof terrace of the place, also designed by Jean Nouvel, allows you to enjoy one of the most beautiful views of Paris.

27 Quai Branly, 7ᵉ. 01 47 53 68 00.
Open daily, noon–2:45pm and 7–10:30pm.
www.lesombres-restaurant.com
No. 07-23 (Quai Branly, 7ᵉ).

COMPTOIRS BOURDONNAIS
Give your wardrobe a new lease on life and succumb to this boutique's exclusive selection of brands that mix "ultra-cool" and "ultra-smart": American Vintage, Humanoid, Bellerose, Velvet, Belstaff… A world of chic casualwear that is in keeping with the area.

41 Av. de la Bourdonnais, 7ᵉ. 01 45 51 22 87.
www.comptoirs-bourdonnais.com
Open Mon, 2–7:15pm; Tue–Sat, 10:30am–7:15pm.
No. 07-24 (43 Av. Rapp, 7ᵉ).

VIN SUR VIN
Looking for an unforgettable experience? Discover a stunning list of 800 wines in this modern design restaurant filled with artwork. A friendly atmosphere is guaranteed and the welcome unequaled.

20 Rue de Monttessuy, 7ᵉ. 01 47 05 14 20.
Open Mon–Sat, noon–1:30pm and 7–9:30pm.
No. 07-24 (43 Av. Rapp, 7ᵉ).

POTTOKA
This bistro, with its creative, Basque-style cuisine, is a true breath of fresh air. But it's very basic – just a bar, some tables, and touches of earthy browns and greens. The dishes are sumptuous, bright and flavourful. And the Basque palette is balanced with a sophisticated culinary history, where friendliness is a must. The set menu – starter, main course, and dessert – costs €35.

4 Rue de l'Exposition, 7ᵉ. 01 45 51 88 38.
www.pottoka.fr – Open daily, noon–2:30pm and 7:30–11pm.
No. 07-21 (37 Av. Bosquet, 7ᵉ).

CHATTANOOGA
Open since 1978, Chattanooga was the first skate-and-surf shop to open in Paris. The founder's daughter has taken over the reins with the same passion to continue her father's vision. Nostalgic traditionalists will be delighted, while younger generations will be surprised … A small corner of California in the heart of Paris!

53 Av. Bosquet, 7ᵉ. 01 45 51 76 65.
www.chattanooga.fr
Open Mon, 3–7:30pm; Tue–Sat, 10:30am–7:30pm.
No. 07-21 (37 Av. Bosquet, 7ᵉ).

LE BARDELO
This jazz club is the "in" place to go out in this rather quiet neighbourhood. Regulars flock to the bar on the ground floor, which has an Art Deco ambience, while jazz concerts are held in the vaulted basement on Saturday nights. People also come here to enjoy a whisky chosen from the many varieties on offer.

64 Av. Bosquet, 7ᵉ. 01 44 18 01 25. Open 6pm–2am.
No. 07-19 (85 Av. Bosquet, 7ᵉ).

LES DEUX ABEILLES
Don't come to this English-style tearoom serving sweet and savoury treats swearing that you're not going to stuff yourself with pastries. It'll be a waste of time – it's all so good!

189 Rue de l'Université, 7ᵉ. 01 45 55 64 04.
Open Mon–Sat, 9am–7pm.
No. 07-22 (3 Av. Bosquet, 7ᵉ).

Calendar of Events

Exhibitions at the Quai Branly Museum
Scan this flashcode or visit
http://blog.velib.paris.fr/
en/?s=museequaibranlyEn

⭐ A Word From Vélib'

Here you are facing the icon of the French capital, admired by visitors from all over the world: the Eiffel Tower. Leave your Vélib' at the large Quai Branly station (07-23). If there are no spaces left there, you can find eight Vélib' stations around Champs-de-Mars.

Eiffel Tower

The tower has 1652 steps, stands 325 m (1066 ft) tall and weighs some 10,100 tonnes: the figures alone are enough to give you vertigo! To test your resistance to altitude, go right to the top. On the second level, glazed windows offer you a bird's eye view of the ground far below. On the third level, you can admire the whole of Paris: the view stretches out before you some 67 km (42 mi). The most visited site in the world, the Eiffel Tower is the undisputed symbol of the capital, designed and inaugurated by Gustave Eiffel for the World Fair of 1889. Don't miss the museum on the first level, and on the ground floor, the tour of the machinery of an 1899 lift. For gourmets, the Eiffel Tower has one of the best restaurants in Paris – Le Jules Verne. Start saving!

5 Av. Anatole-France, 7e. 0 892 70 12 39. www.tour-eiffel.fr
Accessible daily, 9am–11pm (midnight in summer).
🚲 No. 07-23 (Quai Branly, 7e).

Champ-de-Mars

This is the favourite playground of families across the capital. Indeed, it's easy to spend a whole day along this huge expanse dominated by the Eiffel Tower. You can picnic on the lawns while watching amateur jugglers or football players on Sundays.

Or, you could go for a donkey or carousel ride, tackle the swings, go go-karting, or play on one of the many playgrounds.

🚲 No. 07-23 (Quai Branly, 7e).

Pont de Bir-Hakeim

The first metal footbridge, built for the 1878 World Fair, quickly became a victim of its own success. A new bridge had to be designed, called the Passy Viaduct, which could carry pedestrians, cars, and the metro. A 247 m- (810 ft-) long bridge was built: the lower part was 24.2 m (79.4 ft) wide, with two 6m (20 ft) traffic lanes, a central walkway and two sidewalks; the metro ran over the top. The bridge was renamed in 1949 to honour Koenig's victory at Bir-Hakeim, Libya.

🚲 No. 15-26 (6 Bd. de Grenelle, 15e).

Île aux Cygnes

Whatever the time of day, you will feel like you are anywhere except Paris! You can explore the former Grenelle Dike, which is nearly 900 m (3000 ft) long, barely 11 m (36 ft) wide and planted with more than 300 trees (more than 60 different species). To escape the commotion of the city, come find a place by the edge of the Seine, at the foot of the Statue of Liberty, and with the Eiffel Tower in view ahead. The replica of the statue, offered by the city of New York in 1886, was created only three years after the original in a cast by Bartholdi. It is, however, much less famous!

🚲 No. 15-26 (6 Bd. de Grenelle, 15e).

Under the footbridge of the Viaduc de Passy

"Parisian Manhattan" seen from the Île aux Cygnes

Taking a Break

CAFÉ PRIMEROSE
The large brown and beige tiled facade of this café/bistro ushers you into an Art Nouveau-style interior. On sunny days, you can enjoy a glass of wine on its beautiful terrace. And if you're getting hungry, a drink can lead on to dinner, with excellent French cuisine included.

🍽 64 Av. de la Motte-Picquet, 15ᵉ. 01 42 73 20 13.
Ⓥ No. 15-24 (88 Av. de Suffren, 15ᵉ).

ERAWAN
This restaurant won't disappoint lovers of Asian cuisine. Explosions of flavours, not all mouth-searingly hot, are on the menu in this restaurant run by the same Thai family for more than 30 years. The traditional decor and costumes add to the authenticity of the place. Remember to book ahead as Erawan is often full.

🍽 76 Rue de la Fédération, 15ᵉ. 01 47 83 55 67.
Ⓥ No. 15-105 (84 Rue de la Fédération, 15ᵉ).

EIFFEL CLUB
Open only in summer, this club hosts night-revellers on more than 600 m² (6460 ft²) of space, with a huge quayside terrace, a barge, three bars, and two dance floors. People come here for the relaxed atmosphere and the eclectic music. An idyllic setting to dance and relax...

🍽 Port de Suffren, 7ᵉ. 01 77 18 02 49.
Open every Sat, Jun–Sept, 8am–5:30am.
Ⓥ No. 07-25 (2 Av. Octave-Gréard, 7ᵉ).

LE SUFFREN
This lounge bar, which also doubles as a restaurant, transforms into a *salon de thé* and bar in the evening. Those seeking of peace and serenity will be delighted by this charming place, whose welcoming decor was designed by architects Michel and Richard Lafon.

🍽 84 Av. de Suffren, 15ᵉ. 01 45 66 97 86.
Open daily, 7am–11:45pm.
Ⓥ No. 15-24 (88 Av. de Suffren, 15ᵉ).

LE BEAUJOLAIS
Head back in time here through the flavours of the Auvergne. Whether you sit inside or in the sunshine on the terrace, the regional produce of the Auvergne will provide a real change of scene. Cheese, cured meats, *tripoux*, and *truffade* are on the menu, and can be washed down with fine wines.

🍽 28 Av. de Suffren, 15ᵉ. 01 47 83 62 58.
www.lebeaujolais.fr – Open daily, 7am–1am.
Ⓥ No. 15-71 (36 Rue de Suffren, 15ᵉ).

THÉ AUX TROIS CERISES
Spend an afternoon in this romantic little tearoom indulging in homemade hot chocolate, a cappuccino, or a piece of coconut or chocolate cake. This charming spot will revitalize your taste buds with simple sweet treats in a fairytale atmosphere. In the spring and summertime you can enjoy the wonderful little English-style garden.

🍽 47 Av. de Suffren, 7ᵉ. 01 42 73 92 97.
Open Tue–Fri, noon–6pm, Sat and Sun, noon–7pm.
Ⓥ No. 15-105 (84 Rue de la Fédération, 15ᵉ).

29

The Eiffel Tower seen from the Trocadero

Route 2

Paris, City of Light

Explore Paris's Right Bank, from Bastille to the Palais de Chaillot! Catch the incredible perspective of the Champs-Élysées, and end on a high note on the Place du Trocadéro. There, one of the most beautiful views of Paris unfolds in front of you – the Eiffel Tower standing proud ans majestic. A magical route that you can follow at your own pace, in the daytime or after dark. Come night, Paris enrobes itself in a mantle of light ... How romantic and festive!

....

STAGE 1 — BASTILLE TO SAINT-PAUL

⭐ A Word From Vélib' ....

For this itinerary, use the bus lane on the Rue de Rivoli, which is open to cyclists. The first goal in sight: the Maison des Parisiens, also known as the Hôtel de Ville de Paris.

Place de la Bastille

In former days, this was the site of the Bastille, the famous prison of the Ancien Régime, in which the Man in the Iron Mask and later Voltaire and Mirabeau were held. It became the symbol of the French Revolution when, on July 14, 1789, Parisians stormed the fortress and freed the prisoners before levelling it stone by stone. The trendy area around the square is full of bars and clubs.

🚲 No. 11-001 (2 Bd. Richard-Lenoir, 11ᵉ).

Colonne de Juillet

Don't be fooled – the fine column standing in the centre of the Place de la Bastille is not to commemorate the people's storming of the Bastille. Rather, it celebrates the July Revolution, or *Trois Glorieuses*: from July 27 to 29, 1830, the people rose up against Charles X to establish, after the Second Restoration, the July Monarchy. The column, over 47 m (154 ft) high and crowned with the *Génie de la Liberté* (the Spirit of Freedom) – which is reminiscent of Delacroix's famous painting *La Liberté guidant le peuple* – celebrates this bloody episode in the history of France.

🚲 No. 11-001 (2 Bd. Richard-Lenoir, 11ᵉ).

July Column

The gardens of the Place des Vosges

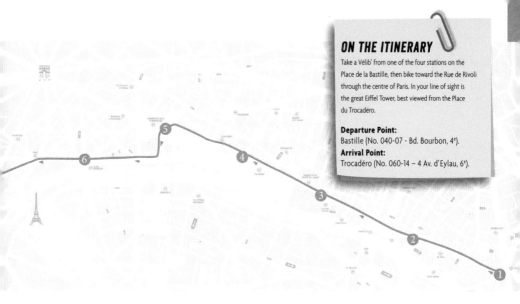

ON THE ITINERARY

Take a Vélib' from one of the four stations on the
Place de la Bastille, then bike toward the Rue de Rivoli
through the centre of Paris. In your line of sight is
the great Eiffel Tower, best viewed from the Place
du Trocadéro.

Departure Point:
Bastille (No. 040-07 - Bd. Bourbon, 4ᵉ).
Arrival Point:
Trocadéro (No. 060-14 - 4 Av. d'Eylau, 6ᵉ).

Place des Vosges

In the heart of the Marais, this square is a beautiful
place in which to stroll. One of the oldest in Paris,
originally known as the Place Royale, it was
conceived by Henri IV and built during the reign of
Louis XIII. Jousting tournaments and other games
were also held here. After the Revolution, it was
named after the first department to pay its taxes: the
Vosges. Some of the greatest names in Parisian life
have met or lived here, including Mme de Sévigné,
Bossuet, Richelieu, and Théophile Gautier.

🅥 No. 04-101 (11 Rue de la Bastille, 4ᵉ).

Victor Hugo's House

One of the Place des Vosges' most famous residents
was Victor Hugo, who lived here from 1832 to 1848,
in the Hôtel de Rohan-Guéménée (17th century).
In the early 20th century, it became a museum
where the writer's home is brought to life. You can
see some of his furniture, as well as documents
tracing the history of his life and work. *Fantastique !*

6 Pl. des Vosges, 4ᵉ. 01 42 72 10 16.
Open Tue–Sun, 10am–5:30pm.
🅥 No. 04-101 (11 Rue de la Bastille, 4ᵉ).

Place du Marché Sainte-Catherine

Park your Vélib' to explore this lovely paved square,
built on the site of the former Sainte-Catherine-du-
Val-des-Écoliers convent, which stood here until the
13th century. The buildings that surround it today,
and their fine layout, date back to the 18th century. In
the centre of the square, white mulberry trees adorn
this charming, rather theatrical setting away from
the hustle and bustle of Rue Saint-Antoine. A lovely
square in which to take a break on a sunny day!

🅥 No. 04-10 (105-109 Terre-Plein Saint-Paul, 4ᵉ).

Église Saint-Paul-Saint-Louis

Take the time to admire the monumental Gothic
facade of this church, which was built at the
instigation of Louis XIII in the 17th century for
the Jesuit order. Its interior architecture, which is
reminiscent of Italy as well as the French Gothic
style, impresses by its height, light, and elongated
proportions. You can also see a work by Delacroix:
Le Christ en agonie au jardin des oliviers. Bossuet
and Bourdaloue both preached here and it was
in this church, too, that Léopoldine Hugo, Victor
Hugo's daughter, got married.

🅥 No. 04-10 (105 Terre-Plein Saint-Paul, 4ᵉ).

PLACE DE
L'ÉTOILE

ST-PHILIPPE
DU ROULE

RUE ST HONORÉ

AV. DES CHAMPS-ÉLYSÉES

08-50

08-32

08-49

08-41

08-39

08-13

08-40

08-31

08-105

FRANKLIN
D. ROOSEVELT

CHAMPS ÉLYSÉES
CLEMENCEAU

AV. D'IÉNA

AV. MARCEAU

AV. GORGE-V

08-48

16-15

08-47

BOISSIÈRE

AV. MONTAIGNE

MUSÉE
GUIMET

08-14

08-14

GRAND
PALAIS

AV. KLÉBER

16-07

IÉNA

MUSÉE
GALLIERA

08-45

08-29

PET
PAL

08-46

COURS ALBERT-1ER

COURS DE LA REINE

TROCADÉRO

AV. DU PRÉSIDENT-WILSON

PALAIS
DE TOKYO

MUSÉE D'ART
MODERNE

PT DE L'ALMA

ALMA
MARCEAU

La Seine

DES INVALIDES

PT ALEXANDRE-III

INVAL

AQUARIUM
DE PARIS

QUAI BRANLY

PALAIS DE
CHAILLOT

PT D'IÉNA

AV. DE LA BOURDONNAIS

CHAMPS
DE MARS

PT DE BIR-HAKEIM

· Théâtre des Champs-Élysées
· Avenue Montaigne
· Pont de l'Alma
· Musée Galliera
· Musée des Arts Asiatiques Guimet

 · Le Plaza Athénée
 · Chez Francis
 · Crazy Horse
 · Le Bar des Théâtres

STAGE 6

· Pont Alexandre-III
· Petit Palais
· Grand Palais
· Palais de la Découverte
· Palais de l'Élysée
· The Champs-Élysées

 · Cafétéria du Petit Palais
 · Mini Palais
 · Théâtre du Rond-Point
 · Showcase
 · Artcurial
 · Paris Saint-Germain
   Boutique Store
 · Levi's
 · Lenôtre

STAGE 5

· Musée d'Art Moderne
· Palais de Tokyo
· Place du Trocadéro
· Palais de Chaillot
· Aquarium de Paris (Ciné-Aqua)

 · Frog XVI
 · Tokyo Eat
 · Schwartz's Deli
 · Le Baron
 · Marché de l'Alma
 · Carette
 · Bert's Alma-Marceau

STAGE 7

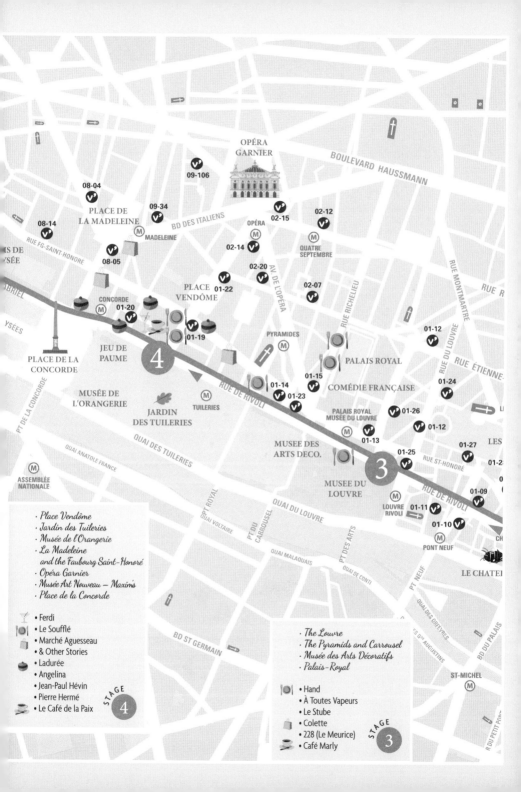

OPÉRA GARNIER

BOULEVARD HAUSSMANN

08-04

PLACE DE LA MADELEINE

09-34

09-106

BD DES ITALIENS

MADELEINE

08-14

RUE FG-SAINT-HONORE

OPÉRA

02-15

02-12

QUATRE SEPTEMBRE

08-05

02-14

02-20

AV DE L'OPERA

02-07

PLACE VENDÔME

01-22

CONCORDE

01-20

01-19

PYRAMIDES

PLACE DE LA CONCORDE

JEU DE PAUME

01-12

01-14

01-23

01-15

PALAIS ROYAL

COMÉDIE FRANÇAISE

01-24

RUE DU LOUVRE

RUE ÉTIENNE

RUE RICHELIEU

RUE MONTMARTRE

MUSÉE DE L'ORANGERIE

JARDIN DES TUILERIES

TUILERIES

RUE DE RIVOLI

PALAIS ROYAL MUSÉE DU LOUVRE

01-26

01-12

01-13

MUSEE DES ARTS DECO.

01-25

01-27

RUE ST-HONORE

LES

QUAI ANATOLE FRANCE

QUAI DES TUILERIES

MUSÉE DU LOUVRE

RUE DE RIVOLI

01-09

ASSEMBLÉE NATIONALE

PT ROYAL

QUAI DU LOUVRE

LOUVRE RIVOLI

01-11

01-10

PT DU CARROUSEL

PT DES ARTS

PONT NEUF

QUAI VOLTAIRE

QUAI MALAQUAIS

QUAI DE CONTI

PT NEUF

LE CHATE

QUAIS GDS AUGUSTINS

BD DU PALAIS

BD ST GERMAIN

ST-MICHEL

R DU PETIT PONT

· Place Vendôme
· Jardin des Tuileries
· Musée de l'Orangerie
· La Madeleine
  and the Faubourg Saint-Honoré
· Opéra Garnier
· Musée Art Nouveau – Maxim's
· Place de la Concorde

• Ferdi
• Le Soufflé
• Marché Aguesseau
• & Other Stories
• Ladurée
• Angelina
• Jean-Paul Hévin
• Pierre Hermé
• Le Café de la Paix

STAGE 4

· The Louvre
· The Pyramids and Carrousel
· Musée des Arts Décoratifs
· Palais-Royal

• Hand
• À Toutes Vapeurs
• Le Stube
• Colette
• 228 (Le Meurice)
• Café Marly

STAGE 3

- Hôtel de Ville de Paris
- Rue de Rivoli
- Le Marais
- Pont des Arts
- Musée Carnavalet
- Musée Picasso
- Le musée d'Art et d'Histoire du Judaïsme
- Église Saint-Eustache
- Les Halles de Paris (Forum des Halles)
- Châtelet
- Centre Pompidou
- Fontaine des Innocents

- Pick Clops
- La Perle
- Le Trésor
- Chez Julien
- Café Clémentine
- Duc des Lombards
- Victoria Cross
- FREE' P'STAR
- Pozzetto
- Comme à Lisbonne
- Mosaïques

STAGE 2

- Place de la Bastille
- Colonne de Juillet
- Place des Vosges
- Victor Hugo's House
- Place du Marché Sainte-Catherine
- Église Saint-Paul-Saint-Louis
- Village Saint-Paul
- Hôtel de Sens (and the Forney Library)

- Sherry But
- CRU
- Breakfast in America
- La Tête Ailleurs
- Le Loir dans la Théière
- Le Café Martini

STAGE 1

Village Saint-Paul

This is the place to find antiques!
A backdrop to Medieval Paris and Charles V's place of residence, Village Saint-Paul shows another side of the Marais.

Antique shops as well as design and contemporary art galleries abound in this area, which stretches between Rue des Jardins-Saint-Paul, Rue Charlemagne, Rue Saint-Paul, and Rue de l'Ave-Maria.

No. 04-10 (105-109 Terre-Plein Saint-Paul, 4ᵉ).

Hôtel de Sens (and the Forney Library)

At no. 1 Rue du Figuier, you will find a castle worthy of the Middle Ages. And in fact it is! Corner turrets, a square tower, a facade with wide ribs and hidden arrow slits, the former residence of the Archibishop of Sens later became the headquarters of the "Messageries, coches et carrosses de Lyon, Bourgogne et Franche-Comté". It was from here that carriages left for Eastern Paris. Since then it has even seen a laundry, an optician, a rabbit grooming service, and Queen Margot as a resident. It was bought by the Mairie de Paris in 1911, and subsequently restored. Today the building houses the Forney Library, dedicated to artistic and decorative craftsmanship. Note: the Hôtel de Sens is not open to the public.

1 Rue du Figuier, 4ᵉ.
No. 40-09 (6 Rue Saint-Paul, 4ᵉ).

 **ALSO WORTH SEEING ON THE WAY**

HÔTEL DE SULLY ★ ★ ★

MUSÉE DE LA MAGIE ★ ★

35

Taking a Break

CRU

A great place for healthy (but not disappointing) meal! Vegetables, fruit, meat and fish can be enjoyed raw. For those who can't do without a hot dish, food can be cooked *à la plancha*.

Village Saint-Paul, 7 Rue Charlemagne, 4ᵉ. 01 40 27 81 84 – www.restaurantcru.fr – Open Tue–Sun
No. 04-10 (105 Terre-Plein Saint-Paul, 4ᵉ).

LE LOIR DANS LA THÉIÈRE

The homemade desserts in this eclectic place are exhibited like trophies on a dresser are known throughout Paris. People will cross the city to enjoy the lemon meringue pie…

3 Rue de Rosiers, 4ᵉ. 01 42 72 90 61. Open daily, 10am–7:30pm.
No. 04-10 (105 Terre-Plein Saint-Paul, 4ᵉ).

BREAKFAST IN AMERICA

You sometimes have to be patient to get into this American diner, but once inside you'll attain culinary nirvana! If you're not counting calories, try the milkshake and the pancakes.

4 Rue Malher, Paris 4ᵉ. 01 42 72 40 21.
www.breakfast-in-america.com – Open daily, 8:30am–11pm.
No. 04-10 (105 Terre-Plein Saint-Paul, 4ᵉ).

LE CAFÉ MARTINI

There's a friendly funky vibe to this quirky place. Collapse on one of the super comfortable couches and enjoy a traditional hot chocolate or homemade mulled wine. Its jazz concerts and €5 cocktails at happy hour have gained it a loyal following.

11 Rue du Pas-de-la-Mule, 4ᵉ.
www.cafemartini.fr – Open Tue–Sat, 6pm–2am.
No. 41-07 (27 Bd. Beaumarchais, 4ᵉ).

SHERRY BUT

Their specialties are cocktails and… whisky! With their 56 varieties, Scotch fans are sure to be pleased.

20 Rue Beautreillis, 4ᵉ. 09 83 38 47 80.
Open Tue-Sat, 6pm-2am.
No. 04-09 (6 Rue Saint-Paul, 4ᵉ).

LA TÊTE AILLEURS

Close your eyes. Listen to the crickets chirping. Ah, no! It's the call of antipasti and other Mediterranean-inspired dishes that make you believe that St-Tropez has relocated to the centre of Paris.

20 Rue Beautreillis, 4ᵉ. 01 42 72 47 80.
www.lateteailleurs.fr
No. 04-09 (6 Rue Saint-Paul, 4ᵉ).

⭐ **A Word From Vélib'** ••••••••••••••••••••••
When you arrive at Hôtel de Ville, drop off your Vélib' so you can stroll around the Marais or go see an exhibition at the Pompidou Centre. Then get back on your bike and continue along the Rue de Rivoli to Les Halles and Châtelet.

Hôtel de Ville de Paris

Some extraordinary things have happened on the Place de l'Hôtel-de-Ville! Originally known as the "Maison aux piliers" (House of Pillars), the building became the seat of the city's municipal institutions in 1357. A place where people came to express themselves, it was in this square, formerly called Place de Grève and renamed in 1830, that unemployed workers used to gather. It was also the rallying point for rioters, insurgents, and revolutionaries. Designed by the Italian architect Boccador in the sixteenth century, the building was rebuilt by Théodore Ballu and Édouard Deperthes, and retained its Neo-Renaissance style after the fire of 1871, during the Paris Commune. And it was from its balconies that General de Gaulle triumphantly uttered his famous words: "Paris! Paris outraged! Paris broken! Paris martyred! But Paris liberated!" Today, you can enjoy free exhibits here about the capital. Always a hit!

29 Rue de Rivoli, 1ᵉʳ. www.paris.fr
🔵 No. 04-16 (3 Rue Lobau, 4ᵉ).

Rue de Rivoli

The 3 km (2 mi) long former Rue Impériale today evokes, with its Italian name, one of Napoleon Bonaparte's victories over Austria, in 1797, during the Italian campaign. The most beautiful stretch of the road is the northern section, which is lined with arcades built during the Second Empire. Today it is home to numerous shops.

Le Marais

Stroll between Rue des Archives, Rue des Francs-Bourgeois, and Rue Vieille-du-Temple to admire the *hôtels particuliers* (mansions) and to enjoy the ambience of Paris's gay district and Jewish quarter. Park your Vélib' at a station if you decide to visit one of the museums located in one of the pretigious homes: the Musée Carnavalet for a walk through the Parisian history; the Musée Cognacq-Jay for its collection of 18th century European art; or the Musée Picasso.

Pont des Arts

This footbridge linking the banks of the Seine is known by lovers everywhere, who come to seal their eternal love here with a lock placed on its metal railings. In the evening, it is very popular with Parisians, who come to picnic on the ground in a romantic atmosphere.
(see also route 1, p. 19)

Between the Quai du Louvre (1ᵉʳ) and the Quai Malaquais (6ᵉ).
🔵 No. 06-01 (5 Quai Malaquais, 6ᵉ).

Musée Carnavalet

The Hôtel Carnavalet is one of the oldest examples of Renaissance architecture in Paris,

Pompidou Centre

Lovers on the Pont des Arts

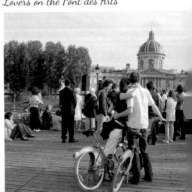

built between 1548 and 1560 for Jacques de Lignerie, a parliamentary president.
An amusing fact: its name is the distortion of that of one of its owners, Mme de Kernevenoy. There's much to enjoy, from Jean Goujon's sculptures to the courtyard ornamentations (inspired by the four seasons and the zodiac signs), as well as the extensions carried out by François Mansart in the late 17th century. Paintings, interior reconstructions, models, and artifacts take you back to the Paris of yesteryear.

23 Rue de Sévigné, 3ᵉ. 01 44 59 58 58.
Open Tue–Sun, 10am–6pm.
Free entry to the permanent collections.
🆅 No. 04-10 (105-109 Terre-Plein Saint-Paul, 4ᵉ).

Musée Picasso

This museum, which has been entirely renovated, holds a collection of works by the artist, but also masterpieces from his private collection, including works by Cézanne, Renoir, and Modigliani. The museum is housed in the splendid Hôtel Salé, which takes its name from the original owner – a farmer who made a fortune on the salt tax!

5 Rue de Thorigny, 3ᵉ. 01 42 71 25 21.
🆅 No. 03-08 (22 Rue de la Perle, 3ᵉ).

Musée d'Art et d'Histoire du Judaïsme

Built by Pierre Le Muet between 1644 and 1650, the building was enlarged by its new owner, the Duke of Saint-Aignan, in 1688. André Le Nôtre, (of Versailles fame) was responsible for the landscaping of the gardens, ponds and parterres. Inside, don't miss the magnificent staircase and the trompe l'œil of the dome. You can still appreciate touches of the old dining room, such as a superb fresco from the mid-17th century. In 1986, the former Hôtel de Saint-Aignan was transformed into the Museum of Jewish Art and History. Special collections, temporary exhibitions, and cultural artifacts are on display to visitors.

71 Rue du Temple, 3ᵉ. 01 53 01 86 53. www.mahj.org. Admission fee. 🆅 No. 03-09 (76 Rue du Temple, 3ᵉ).

Église Saint-Eustache

The architecture of this church, built between 1532 and 1667, is, to say the least, complex but fascinating, with Gothic elements on the exterior, a Renaissance interior, and a Classical facade. An interesting fact: St. Eustache is the patron saint of hunters.

2 Impasse Saint-Eustache, 1ᵉʳ.
🆅 No. 10-08 (Porte Saint-Eustache, Rue Rambuteau, 1ᵉʳ).

Les Halles de Paris (Forum des Halles)

Enter the anthill at the heart of Paris! This huge shopping area, half of which is underground, was created on the site of the former large central wholesale marketplace and receives 800,000 people every day and more than 40 million visitors a year. In 2010, renovations were begun to restructure the transportation system, build a new garden, and redevelop the shopping mall, with a canopy overlooking the garden.
Further additions include the newly refurbished Forum des Images, a conservatory, and a hip-hop school.

01 44 76 96 56. www.forumdeshalles.com
Open daily, 10am–8pm.
🆅 No. 10-27 (29 Rue Berger, 1ᵉʳ).

Châtelet

Standing in the middle of the Place du Châtelet with its Fontaine du Palmier, you have on one side the Théâtre du Châtelet, Paris's musical theatre, and on the other, the Théâtre de la Ville, formerly the Théâtre Sarah-Bernhardt. Nearby, you will find the Tour Saint-Jacques, the old steeple of a Gothic-style church, built in the 16th century and which was demolished in 1802. It was the assembly and departure point for the Saint-Jacques-de-Compostelle (Way of St. James) pilgrimage. From 1891, the tower was home

Calendar of Events
The Free exhibitions at the l'Hôtel de Ville de Paris
Scan this flashcode or visit
http://blog.velib.paris.fr/en/?s=hoteldevilleEN

37

to a weather station, whose data were used by the Montsouris observatory.

🚇 No. 10-02 (14 Av. Victoria, 1ᵉʳ).

Pompidou Centre

Its glass walls and imposing steel framework give the centre the appearance of a factory. Inaugurated in 1977 by President Georges Pompidou, the museum is both fascinating and controversial. It houses the Musée National d'Art Moderne (MNAM), the Bibliothèque Publique d'Information (BPI, a vast public library), IRCAM (a centre for music and acoustic research), galleries for temporary exhibits, and performance venues (for cinema, dance, music, and theatre). Over the years it has become a major space for contemporary art, that is internationally acclaimed and much visited.

3 Rue Beaubourg, 4ᵉ. 01 44 78 12 33.
www.centrepompidou.fr
🚇 No. 04-21 (46 Rue Beaubourg, 4ᵉ).

Taking a Break

Fontaine des Innocents

On the Place Joachim-du-Bellay, surrounded by shops teeming with curious browsers, stands a statue created by sculptor Jean Goujon (1510–1566), which celebrates the arrival of Henri II in Paris. The square that hosts it is a well-known crossing and meeting point for Parisians.

At the corner of Rue Saint-Denis and Rue Berger, 1ᵉʳ.
🚇 No. 10-05 (3 Rue de la Cossonerie, 1ᵉʳ).

 **ALSO WORTH SEEING ON THE WAY**

MUSÉE COGNACQ-JAY ★

MUSÉE DE L'HISTOIRE DE FRANCE ★ ★

PLACE ET LA FONTAINE STRAVINSKY ★

ÉGLISE SAINT-MERRI ★ ★

PICK CLOPS

With its retro 1950s style interior, where you might bump into Pete Doherty, Pick Clops looks like a classic bar from the outside. It shuns tourists, but there's always a spot on the terrace where you can enjoy the sun.

🍸 16 Rue Vieille-du-Temple, 4ᵉ. 01 40 29 02 18.
Open daily, 8am–2am (Sun, 9:30am–midnight).
🚇 No. 04-15 (25 Rue du Pont-Louis-Philippe, 4ᵉ).

LE TRÉSOR

A little gem of a restaurant/bar with a neo-chic Italian feel to its baroque decor. French cuisine marries with Italian in its delicious pizzas and other traditional dishes. On the drinks front, try out the delicious mulled wine.

🍽 7 Rue du Trésor, 3ᵉ. 01 42 71 35 17. Open daily, noon–1am.
🚇 No. 04-13 (50 Rue Vieille-du-Temple, 4ᵉ).

FREE'P'STAR

This is one of the busiest second-hand clothes stores in the Marais, with a good selection of vin-

tage dresses, skirts and shirts. It's especially worth a visit for its boots and its Russian-print scarves. As a bonus: the dresses sell for between 10 and €20 and the military shirts and jackets for €10.

8 Rue Sainte-Croix-de-la-Bretonnerie, 4ᵉ. 01 42 76 03 72. www.freepstar.com – Open daily, noon–9pm

No. 04-19 (4 Rue du Cloître-Saint-Merri, 4ᵉ).

POZZETTO

Come and enjoy a good Italian gelato ice cream (made with whole milk rather than cream) that tastes like no ice cream you've ever had before. Pozzetto offers only a dozen flavours in order to keep them fresh. Even better, in the summer, why not enjoy your ice cream with your feet up, relaxing on a sun lounger at Paris Plages?

39 Rue du Roi-de-Sicile, 4ᵉ. 01 42 77 08 64. www.pozzetto.biz – No. 41-03 (1 Rue des Archives, 4ᵉ).

DUC DES LOMBARDS

This legendary club from the 1980s has seen some jazz greats. Musical freedom allows artists to come and share their music with an informed audience or to face other musicians in jam sessions.

42 Rue des Lombards, 1ᵉʳ. 01 42 33 22 88. www.ducsdeslombards.com – Concerts Mon–Sat, 8–10pm.

No. 01-03 (7 Rue Saint-Denis, 1ᵉʳ).

CHEZ JULIEN

A romantic, chic terrace a stone's throw from the Église Saint-Gervais that looks like a filmset of "authentic" old-style Paris, in a real old-Paris style filmset, with its paved alley, little marble tables and assortment of dark grey chairs. Its the most sought-after terrace in Paris by PAF journalists and Parisians making merry.

1 Rue du Pont-Louis-Philippe, Paris 4ᵉ. 01 42 78 31 64. Open daily. No. 04-11 (18 Rue de l'Hôtel-de-Ville, 4ᵉ).

CAFÉ CLÉMENTINE

A nice little café and bistro with a cozy atmosphere, wine bar, traditional cooking, and regional produce. The charcuterie from the Auvergne is excellent and the cheeses tasty. Set menu of starter, main course, and dessert for €27. Bonuses are the direct broadcasting of football and rugby matches and the music that sometimes continues until 2am.

4 Rue de la Coutellerie, 4ᵉ. 09 83 20 87 68. www.cafeclementine.com – Open Mon–Sat, noon–11pm.

No. 04-18 (1 Rue Saint-Bon, 4ᵉ).

LA PERLE

For some mysterious reason, this bar has become the "in" watering hole in which to show up and show off your designer sneakers. When Fashion Week arrives in the City of Light, it becomes impossible to set foot in here: there's no space to be had either inside or outside on the terrace.

78 Rue Vieille-du-Temple, 3ᵉ. 01 42 72 69 93. Open daily, 7am–2am. No. 03-08 (22 Rue de la Perle, 3ᵉ).

COMME À LISBONNE

As its name suggests, this lovely little shop sells typical Portuguese products: olive oil, sardines, chocolate… But the ultimate pleasure, the star of the place, is *the pastel de nata*, a crisp puff pastry filled with light and fluffy cream and served warm. Several batches are baked daily to satisfy the long lines of fans!

37 Rue du Roi-de-Sicile, 4ᵉ. 07 61 23 42 30. www.commealisbonne.com – Open Tue–Sun, 11am–7pm.

No. 41-03 (1 Rue des Archives, 4ᵉ).

VICTORIA CROSS

A contemporary brasserie that is both classic and offbeat, with a sort of bourgeoise punk-rock ambience. Yes, really – that's how the regulars describe it! On "Rock my Thursday", the house DJ entertains. And from Tuesday to Saturday (6pm-midnight), they serve amazing pizzas.

23 Av. Victoria, 1ᵉʳ. 01 40 26 15 68. www.victoria-cross.fr – Open Tue–Sat, 11am–11:30pm.

No. 01-02 (14 Av. Victoria, 1ᵉʳ).

MOSAÏQUES

A small corner of New York in Paris! For €3.50, enjoy a yummy hot-dog with soft bread, chicken sausage, awesome onions, and all kinds of toppings. The homemade onion purée is especially good, as is the typically American sweet mustard.

56 Rue du Roi-de-Sicile, 4ᵉ. 09 77 74 04 85. Open daily, noon–midnight.

No. 41-03 (1 Rue des Archives, 4ᵉ).

39

Calendar of Events
Current exhibitions
at the Pompidou Centre
Scan this flashcode or visit
http://blog.velib.paris.fr/
en/?s=centrepompidouEN

⭐ A Word From Vélib' ·····················
Explore the most beautiful section of the Rue de Rivoli. On the left, you'll see the Louvre, and on the right, the arcades. It's magical at night.

The Louvre

Originally the residence of the France's kings and emperors, the Louvre opened its doors to the public after the Revolution, in 1793. The *Venus de Milo*, the *Mona Lisa*, and *La Liberté guidant le peuple*: so many masterpieces in one palace, the vestiges of which you can still discover. In the Denon, Napoleon, and Sully Wings, choose between Ancient Greek, Roman, Etruscan, Egyptian art, and European paintings. And notice the new "flying carpet", a spectacular steel mesh floating above the Islamic Arts section. Regular visitors take advantage of late-night openings (Wed and Fri until 9:45pm) to be practically alone in the museum's galleries.

There are many entrances, the main ones being via the Napoleon Courtyard and at 99 Rue de Rivoli, 1ᵉʳ. 01 40 20 50 50. www.louvre.fr – Closed Tuesday. Ⓥ No. 01-25 (2 Rue de l'Oratoire, 1ᵉʳ).

The Pyramids and Carrousel

In 1980, a glass pyramid and a pool took their place in the middle of the Napoleon Courtyard. This spectacular entrance, made entirely from glass to reflect the sky, draws tourists from around the world, who enter here to discover the secrets of the Louvre. For a view that stretches out to the Arche de la Défense, go to the Arc de Triomphe du Carrousel, in the axis of the pyramid. Around

Christmastime, you can take a ride on the Big Wheel in the Jardin des Tuileries for an incredible view of monumental Paris.

·☼· Ⓥ No. 01-25 (2 Rue de l'Oratoire, 1ᵉʳ).

Musée des Arts Décoratifs

On the Rue de Rivoli side of the Louvre lies one of the finest collections in the world, in the Musée des Arts Décoratifs, which includes the Musée de la Publicité and the Musée de la Mode et du Textile.

107 Rue de Rivoli, 1ᵉʳ. 01 44 55 57 50. www.lesartsdecoratifs.fr – Open 11am–6pm. Closed Mon. Ⓥ No. 01-14 (12 Rue des Halles, 1ᵉʳ).

Palais-Royal

In hommage to Richelieu, Lemercier designed this 17th-century palace, known as the Palais Cardinal. To-day it houses major institutions of the State. Pass under the archways to access the *cour d'honneur* (forecourt), with its garden surrounded by galleries and famous Buren columns. The novelist Colette and poet Jean Cocteau both lived here once. On the Place Colette, you will see the Kiosque des Noctambules, an unusual metro entrance made from coloured glass beads.

Ⓥ No. 01-13 (186 Rue Saint-Honoré, 1ᵉʳ).

 ALSO WORTH SEEING ON THE WAY

ÉGLISE SAINT-GERMAIN-L'AUXERROIS ★★
COMÉDIE-FRANÇAISE ★★★
GALERIE VÉRO-DODAT ★★

The columns of the Comédie-Française

Taking a Break

HAND

This is the hidden gem in an area full of Asian restaurants. Since opening, the line to enjoy a cheeseburger hasn't diminished. You can choose from different accompaniments: French fries, salad, coleslaw, or hash browns. And when it comes to dessert, the cheesecake and key lime pieare to die for.

📍 39 Rue de Richelieu, 1er. 01 40 15 03 27. Open Tue–Sat. 🚲 No. 01-15 (2 Pl. André-Malraux, 1er).

À TOUTES VAPEURS

The challenge this restaurant has set itself is to allow customers to eat real food quickly and healthily in a friendly atmosphere. You can still take your time to enjoy the balanced and varied food on offer here, you just won't have to wait ages to be served.

📍 2 Rue de l'Échelle, 1er. 01 44 90 95 75. www.atoutesvapeurs.com – Open Mon–Sat, 11am–11pm. 🚲 No. 01-14 (5 Rue de l'Échelle, 1er).

COLETTE

Colette has been reinventing shopping and purveying the latest trends through the seasons and its different designs since 1997. From fashion to literature via cosmetics, design, the latest hi-tech gadgets, and music, this iconic concept store will fulfill the fashionista's every desire as well as delighting casual browsers.

🛍 213 Rue Saint-Honoré, 1er. 01 55 35 33 90. www.colette.fr – Open Mon–Sat, 11am–7pm. 🚲 No. 01-17 (215 Rue Saint-Honoré, 1er).

228 (LE MEURICE)

This bar, with its warm and historical ambience, is one of the best places to enjoy an original cocktail in Paris. Great names such as Dalí and the King of Spain, Alphonse III, were regulars here, but beware of the bill, which could quickly dampen your desires. That said, for the price of a cocktail (€24–30), you will also be able to feast your ears on live jazz from 7pm to midnight.

🍸 228 Rue de Rivoli, 1er. 01 44 58 10 66. Open daily, 11:45am–1:30pm. 🚲 No. 01-18 (2 Rue d'Alger, 1er).

CAFÉ MARLY

Need a little break after visiting the Louvre? Tucked in a corner of the famous palace, Café Marly welcomes you in its modern, wood-panelled decor. The food is good, and there's a lovely terrace overlooking the Place du Carrousel-du-Louvre. The average bill per person is around 40€, but you will be eating at the heart of the Louvre, and you can't put a price on that!

☕ 📍 Pl. du Carrousel, 93 Rue de Rivoli, 1er. 01 49 26 06 60. 🚲 No. 01-23 (161 Rue Saint-Honoré, 1er).

LE STUBE

The self-proclaimed temple of snacking! The *currywurst* is Berlin's iconic sausage dish. At Le Stube, you'll find the Parisian version: pure, unfatty beef, poached and covered in a curried vegetable sauce, accompanied by a salt-crusted baked potato. And for dessert, sachertorte or strudel. Not very good for dieters, but extremely yummy!

📍 31 Rue de Richelieu, 1er. 01 42 60 09 85. Open Mon, 10am–3:30pm; Tue–Sat, 10am–10pm. 🚲 No. 01-15 (2 Pl. André-Malraux, 1er).

Calendar of Events
Plays being performed at the Comédie-Française
Scan this flashcode or visit http://blog.velib.paris.fr/en/?s=comediefrancaiseEN

✹ A Word From Vélib'

As you approach the Champs-Élysées, luxury will increasingly follow in your wake. Use the bike lane of Rue de Rivoli to meander between the luxury hotels and the boutiques of big fashion houses.

Place Vendôme

Away from the bustle streets, Place Vendôme stands grandly as the centre for jewellers. This octagonal square, designed by Hardouin-Mansart in 1699 at Louis XIV's request, features a Trojan Column similar to the one in Rome. It glorifies Napoleon's exploits at Austerlitz, with a statue of Napoleon symbolizing a modern-day Ceasar. Not far from here is the Place de l'Opéra, where converge, among other streets, the prestigious Avenue de l'Opéra and the famous (from the French version of Monopoly, at least) Rue de la Paix, with its equally famous Café de la Paix.

🆅 No. 01-19 (237 Rue Saint-Honoré, 1er).

Jardin des Tuileries

Classed as an historic monument in 1914, this is the oldest French-style garden in Paris. Catherine de Medicis commissioned the garden in 1564, and it was installed on the site of a former tile manufacturer. It's the setting for many events as well as a sculpture park. In the opposite corners of the garden on the Place de la Concorde side, are the Galerie Nationale du Jeu de Paume and the Musée de l'Orangerie.

The Jeu de Paume, which formerly housed real tennis (jeu de paume, the forerunner of Basque pelota and later lawn tennis) courts, has become an exhibition and events venue devoted to photography and video.

Pl. de la Concorde, 1er.
🆅 No. 01-18 (2 Rue d'Alger, 1er).

Musée de l'Orangerie

In 1852, Firmin Bourgeois created this stone and glass building to house the orange trees of the Jardin des Tuileries. In the early 20th century, Monet chose the place to exhibit his *Water Lilies*, on the good advice of his friend Clemenceau. In 1964, the museum received the important Walter-Guillaume collection, which had been donated to the State. Enjoy the Orangerie's Impressionist and post-Impressioninst masterworks; or take in one of the temporary exhibits as well.

In the Jardin des Tuileries. 01 44 77 80 07. Open Wed–Mon, 9am–6pm. Admission fee – www.musee-orangerie.fr
🆅 No. 01-18 (2 Rue d'Alger, 1er).

🕊 **ALSO WORTH SEEING ON THE WAY**

GALERIE NATIONALE DU JEU DE PAUME ★ ★

42

Jardin des Tuileries

Place Vendôme

La Madeleine and the Faubourg Saint-Honoré

The Madeleine church has quite an intriguing history. It took 59 years to build, and it was used alternately as a church or pagan temple, following the ideas of the government of the day. Facing the church, the Rue Royale has its sights on the Place de la Concorde and, on the other side of the Seine, the Palais Bourbon. If you wish, you can take a short diversion to stroll along the Rue du Faubourg-Saint-Honoré in pursuit of Parisian luxury, and to see the Palais de l'Élysée, the official residence of the President of the Republic.

Église de la Madeleine, 4 Rue de Surène, 8ᵉ.
Ⓥ No. 08-05 (4 Pl. de la Madeleine, 8ᵉ).

Opéra Garnier

Named after its architect, Charles Garnier, this opera house was commissioned by Napoleon III and opened in 1875. When Empress Eugénie, looking over the architect's plans, expressed surprise to see that they followed no defined style, Garnier replied felicitiously: "It's neither Greek nor Roman, it's Napoleon III!" In fact, it's a mixture of Baroque and Neo-Renaissance. The interior staircase is majestic, with polychrome steps; there is marble, gilding, and mosaic everywhere; and, last but not least, a Chagall ceiling, created in 1964.

Place de l'Opéra, 9ᵉ. 0892 89 90 90.
www.operadeparis.fr
Ⓥ No. 91-06 (3 Rue Boudreau, 9ᵉ).

Musée Art Nouveau – Maxim's

The famous designer Pierre Cardin, also owner of the restaurant Maxim's, enjoyed collecting Art Nouveau (1900) style artifacts, furniture, and interior accessories, which he exhibits in 12 rooms.

3 Rue Royale, 8ᵉ. 01 42 65 30 47. Open Wed–Sun. Guided tours by reservation at 2pm, 3:15pm, and 4:30pm. Admission fee.
Ⓥ No. 80-05 (6 Pl. de la Madeleine, 8ᵉ).

Place de la Concorde

At the centre of the Place de la Concorde – the grandest in Paris at more than eight hectares (20 acres) – rises an obelisk where the guillotine of the Revolution once stood. A tribute to Ramses II, the obelisk from the Temple of Luxor was given to France by Egypt's Viceroy, and placed on the Concorde by Louis-Philippe in 1830. On this former Place de la Révolution, the guillotine chopped off 1119 heads, including those of Louis XVI and Marie-Antoinette. Also formerly called Place Louis-XV, the square links the Tuileries with the Champs-Élysées, as well as the Palais Bourbon to its architectural counterpart, the Église de la Madeleine. You will see two buildings with twin facades: the famous Hôtel Crillon and the Hôtel de la Marine.

Ⓥ No. 01-20 (2 Rue Cambon, 1ᵉʳ).

Calendar of Events
Extend your trip toward Opéra and the department stores
Scan this flashcode or visit
http://blog.velib.paris.fr/en/?s=operagrandsmagasinsEN

The Columns of La Madeleine

CAFÉ DE LA PAIX

Right by the Opéra Garnier, you'll find an historic terrace offering a great place for a summer drink. Opened in 1962, the Café de la Paix has retained its Second Empire style, with listed frescoes and gilding. It was in the basement here that, in 1896, the first cinematographic film screenings took place. They cost one franc and lasted for four hours! Maupassant and Zola were regulars.

☕ 5 Pl. de l'Opéra, 9ᵉ. 01 40 07 36 36. Open daily.

🚇 No. 20-15 (25 Rue Louis-Le-Grand, 9ᵉ).

LADURÉE

World-renowned pâtissier, Ladurée is the king of *macarons*! Enjoy them in the comfortable *salon de thé* accompanied by a creamy hot chocolate. And to delight you further, there are other irresistible treats on offer, including a yummy strawberry-pistachio *St-Honoré*.

🍰 16 Rue Royale, 8ᵉ. 01 42 60 21 79.

www.laduree.fr

Open Mon–Sat, 8:30am–7pm; Sun, 10am–7pm.

🚇 No. 08-05 (4 Pl. de la Madeleine, 8ᵉ).

AGUESSEAU MARKET

In this area of chic, high-priced fashion boutiques, it's not easy to buy food, other than at Hédiard and Fauchon, for those with expensive tastes. Luckily, there is a little market, whose dozen traders set out their stalls under the colonnades of the Place de la Madeleine.

🏬 Pl. de la Madeleine. Open Tue and Fri, 7am–1:30pm.

🚇 No. 08-04 (4 Bd. Malesherbes, 8ᵉ).

FERDI

It's worth pedalling here to drink the best cocktail in Paris. This friendly little bar, with games up on the walls, serves the best Bloody Mary to be found anywhere in the capital.

🍸 32 Rue du Mont-Thabor, 1ᵉʳ. 01 42 60 82 52.

Open daily, 6:30am–11:15pm.

🚇 No. 01-20 (2 Rue Cambon, 1ᵉʳ).

LE SOUFFLÉ

A stone's throw from Concorde, this restaurant has an old-France ambience, with white tablecloths and traditionally dressed waiters – a nice change from trendy interiors. Try the soufflé menu.

🍽 36 Rue du Mont-Thabor, 1ᵉʳ. 01 42 60 27 19.

www.lesouffle.fr – Open Mon–Sat.

🚇 No. 01-20 (2 Rue Cambon, 1ᵉʳ).

& OTHER STORIES

Here you'll ind a wide range of shoes, bags, accessories, beauty products, and women's clothes. The T-shirts and other clothes are meant to last, as the store's aim is to create a wardrobe with perennial appeal. And there's something for every budgets.

🛍 277 Rue Saint-Honoré, 8ᵉ.

🚇 No. 08-05 (4 Pl. de la Madeleine, 8ᵉ).

ANGELINA

Have a hot chocolate prepared with bars of melted chocolate; it's called an *Africain* and goes very well with a nice homemade *sablé* (shortbread biscuit). Very thick and more creamy than milky, it's a chocaholic's fantasy.

🍰 226 Rue de Rivoli, 1ᵉʳ. 01 42 60 82 00.

www.angelina-paris.fr – Open daily, 8:30am–7pm.

🚇 No. 01-18 (2 Rue d'Alger, 1ᵉʳ).

JEAN-PAUL HÉVIN

Savour the chocolates at Jean-Paul Hévin's, the master of extra-dark ganache and the creator of *chocolats dynamiques*. He is also an *orangettes* expert, and has designed over 20 sumptuous chocolate bars.

🍫 231 Rue Saint-Honoré, 1ᵉʳ. 01 55 35 35 96.

www.jeanpaulhevin.com – Open Mon–Sat, 10am–7:30pm

🚇 No. 01-19 (237 Rue Saint-Honoré, 1ᵉʳ).

PIERRE HERMÉ

Buy your *macarons* here – they're delicious and utterly irresistible. The fame of Hermé's cakes can almost make you forget the excellence, orginality, and creaminess of his chocolates, not to mention his wonderful *tarte au citron*.

🍰 4 Rue Cambon, 1ᵉʳ. 01 43 54 47 77

www.pierreherme.com – Open daily, 10am–7:30pm.

🚇 No. 01-20 (2 Rue Cambon, 1ᵉʳ).

5 THE CHAMPS-ÉLYSÉES

⭐ A Word From Vélib'

Bravo, you've cycled up the 3 km (2 mi) Rue de Rivoli! Now take the most famous avenue in the world: the Champs-Élysées. To cross the Place de la Concorde on your Vélib', it's wise to stay on the outside of it so that you're further away from the cars. You will pass in front of the Hôtel de Crillon and the American Embassy, reaching the Champs-Élysées gardens via Avenue Gabriel.

Pont Alexandre-III

The Alexander III bridge symbolizes the Franco-Russian relations sealed by Czar Alexander III in 1891. Its first stone was laid in 1896 by Czar Nicholas II. Built in three years and opened for the World Fair of 1900, the bridge is made entirely of metal and is composed of a single arch 107.5 m (353 ft) long, which facilitates river traffic and respects the surrounding landscape. *La Renommée tenant Pégase* (Fame Restraining Pegasus) overlooks the capital at the top of the four columns flanking the bridge, and at the base are depicted Charlemagne's France, contemporary France, Renaissance France, and Louis XIV's France. This bridge is so majestic that it would be a sin not to use it to cross over to the Left Bank.

🚲 No. 80-29 (1 Av. Franklin-Roosevelt, 8e).

Petit Palais

The Musée des Beaux-Arts de la Ville de Paris is a place that deserves to be better known. Built for the World Fair of 1900, this delicate building with newly restored ceiling frescoes, is breathtakingly beautiful.

The works on display here are from quite different backgrounds (Ancient Greece, the Renaissance, Paris 1900, etc.), but all contribute to a certain classical elegance.

Av. Winston-Churchill, 8e. 01 53 43 40 00.
Open Tue–Sun, 10am–6pm.
🚲 No. 08-01 (av. Dutuit, 8e).

Grand Palais

Are you a science and architecture buff? Then come inside! The Grand Palais includes the Galeries Nationales and the Palais de la Découverte. In the former are held, with famous artists sometimes accepting, temporary exhibitions, where renowned artists sometimes accept the challenge of creating a work to fit the dimensions of the space. It is also hosts events such as Nuit Électro and FIAC (an international contemporary art fair). The building is truly spectacular, with its glass-roofed nave – the largest in Europe. Exit the building, cross the road, and enter the Palais de la Découverte, which is devoted to science and its applications. It's fascinating and children are welcome.

3 Av. du Général-Eisenhower, 8e. 01 44 13 17 17.
www.grandpalais.fr
🚲 No. 08-29 (1 Av. Franklin-Roosevelt, 8e).

45

Petit Palais

Grand Palais

Palais de la Découverte

This amazing place has devoted itself to the popularization of science since 1931. It appeals to young and old alike.

Av. Franklin-Roosevelt, 8ᵉ. 01 56 43 20 20.
Sun and public holidays, 10am–7pm. Admission fee.
 No. 08-29 (1 Av. Franklin-Roosevelt, 8ᵉ).

ALSO WORTH SEEING ON THE WAY

HÔTEL DE LA MARINE ★ ★

Calendar of Events
**Events and exhibitions
on the Champs-Élysées**
Scan this flashcode or visit
http://blog.velib.paris.fr/en/
?s=champselyseesEN

Palais de l'Élysée

"*Allons enfants de la patri-i-e*"!
Since 1874, the Palais de l'Élysée has been the official residence of the President of the Republic. Built for the Count of Évreux in 1718, it was inherited by the Marquise de Pompadour in 1753, then, in 1808, became the residence of the Emperor and the Empress Josephine.

55 Rue du Faubourg-Saint-Honoré 8ᵉ.
 No. 08-31 (2 Rue Jean-Mermoz, 8ᵉ).

The Champs-Élysées

The world's most beautiful avenue! From the business world to the luxury department stores, via the theatre and great restaurants, it is brimming with activities and offers an exceptional ride from the Arc de Triomphe to the Place de la Concorde. It has also become a gathering place for the Bastille Day (July 14) and for major national events.

Taking a Break

THÉÂTRE DU ROND-POINT

This theatre offers to staging an eclectic and original program featuring contemporary works. It also has a restaurant.

🚋 2 Bis Avenue Franklin-Roosevelt, 8ᵉ. 01 44 95 98 00. www.theatredurondpoint.fr
🅥 No. 08-31 (2 Rue Jean-Mermoz, 8ᵉ).

CAFÉTÉRIA DU PETIT PALAIS

A café with good sandwiches, pâtisseries, ice cream and tea from Mariage Frères. In the summer, you can enjoy all this looking out onto a garden planted with palm trees.

🍽 Av. Winston-Churchill, 8ᵉ. 01 53 43 40 00. Open Tue–Sun, 10am–6pm.
🅥 No. 08-01 (av. Dutuit, 8ᵉ).

ARTCURIAL

Beneath its high wood-panelled ceilings, this bookstore is packed with highly specialist art books: it's here you'll unearth new and second-hand works on modern art, architecture, graphic design and photography that you won't find anywhere else.

📗 7 Rond-Point des Champs-Élysées, 8ᵉ. www.artcurial.com Open Mon–Sat, 11am–7pm. 01 42 99 20 20.
🅥 No. 08-31 (2 Rue Jean-Mermoz, 8ᵉ).

LENÔTRE

Not cheap but divinely decadent. We love this relaxing place with refined taste a stone's throw from the Champs-Élysées. Choose the Lenôtre terrace for its tranquillity, its fine deli dishes, and delicious iced macarons.

🍽 10 Av. des Champs-Élysées, 8ᵉ. 01 42 65 97 70. www.lenotre.com – Open Tue–Sat, noon–10pm.
🅥 No. 08-01 (av. Dutuit, 8ᵉ).

SHOWCASE

Don't miss the Alexander III Bridge, opened for the World Fair of 1900: its single-arch steel bridge symbolizes Franco-Russian relations. Its piers shelter Showcase, a club housed in a former boathouse: sometimes a nightclub, sometimes a concert venue or a television set, it is, in all its various guises, an iconic place of Parisian nightlife.

🚋 Port des Champs-Élysées, 8ᵉ. 01 45 61 25 43. www.showcase.fr – 🅥 No. 01-20 (2 Rue Cambon, 8ᵉ).

MINI PALAIS

The only thing mini about this restaurant is its name: a solid bronze door and impressive volumes make the decor of this restaurant unlike any other. The menu created by a three-starred chef remains fairly simple and offers authentic dishes made with good-quality produce.

🍽 3 Av. Winston-Churchill, 8ᵉ. 01 42 56 42 42. www.minipalais.com – Open daily, 10am–2am.
🅥 No. 08-29 (1 Av. Franklin-Roosevelt, 8ᵉ).

PARIS SAINT-GERMAIN BOUTIQUE STORE

It's impossible to ignore the Parisian temple to the local football club: located on the world's most famous avenue, it's entirely devoted to PSG. Here it's about Paris, and Paris is magic! You'll find every form of merchandise possible or imaginable.

🛍 27 Av. des Champs-Élysées, 8ᵉ. 01 56 69 22 22. www.boutiquepsg.fr – Open daily, 10am–10pm (Sun 8pm).
🅥 No. 08-13 (24 Rue de Marignan, 8ᵉ).

LEVI'S

Admit it, you've never found your perfect pair of jeans, the ones that will give you your dream figure; you abandon them one after another at the back of your wardrobe. This workshop allows customers to have their clothes altered and customized by a team of expert tailors.

🛍 76 Av. des Champs-Élysées, 8ᵉ. 01 53 53 05 70. www.levi.com – Open Mon–Sat, 10am–10pm (Sun 9pm).
🅥 No. 08-41 (16 Rue de Lincoln, 8ᵉ).

Calendar of Events
Trendy boutiques and information about Fashion Week
Scan this flashcode or visit http://blog.velib.paris.fr/en/ ?s=fashionweekEN

⭐ A Word From Vélib'

After a possible pause to shop on the Champs-Élysées, set off again on your Vélib' and head for the Seine. Cycle between the Grand Palais and the Petit Palais along Avenue Winston-Churchill and take the first right to continue alongside the Seine on Cours La-Reine. Keep going straight ahead, under the area's lovely trees, until you reach Place de l'Alma.

Théâtre des Champs-Élysées

At no. 15 of the prestigious Avenue Montaigne stands this immaculate theatre. Built in 1913, in a new quarter conceived by eager of property developers, it was intended to entertain the public by offering them dance performances and concerts. The exterior bas-relief is by Bourdelle, while Denis, Vuillard, and Roussel provided interior decoration. Since its inception, the theatre has consistently offered avant-garde productions to its audiences. The "Gala des Étoiles du XXIᵉ siècle" is one of its proudest achievements. Mixing *pas de deux* from the classical ballet repetoire and contemporary pieces, star dancers from all over the world come to Paris for just four days to enthrall and elevate its spectators.

15 Av. Montaigne, 8ᵉ. 01 49 52 50 50.
www.theatrechampselysees.fr
🅥 No. 08-45 (3 Av. Montaigne, 8ᵉ).

Avenue Montaigne

The quintessential chic and luxurious avenue. From Place de l'Alma to the Champs-Élysées roundabout, Avenue Montaigne is one of the centres of Paris fashion. It was here that Christian Dior set up after the World War II, and its the place to find all the greatest names. The avenue is also famous for the luxury hotel, the Plaza Athénée and the Théâtre des Champs-Élysées.

🅥 No. 08-45 (3 Av. Montaigne, 8ᵉ).

Pont de l'Alma

It was here that Diana, Princess of Wales, was tragically killed in an accident in late August 1997. Overlooking the bridge tunnel, the Flame of Liberty – an exact replica of that of the statue in New York, which was offered to France in 1989 – has since turned into a "Lady Di Memorial". On a less sad note, you will notice the statue of the Zouave, sheltered by the Pont de l'Alma. It's a real barometer: when the water level of the Seine rises to his thighs, it is said that the river is no longer navigable. In 1910, the year of the Great Flood of Paris, the water reached his chin!

🅥 No. 08-45 (3 Av. Montaigne, 8ᵉ).

Musée Galliera

Followers of fashion and lovers of rare fabrics and beautiful cuts take note! Housed in a Renaissance-style palace built by the Duchess of Galliera in the late 19th century, this museum's mandate is to bring to life the major pieces of fashion history and contemporary wear. An unforgettable journey into the world of clothing.

10 Av. Pierre-1er-de-Serbie, 16e. 01 56 52 86 00.

V No. 16-07 (4 Rue de Longchamp, 16e).

Musée des Arts Asiatiques Guimet

Initially, Émile Guimet's collection was housed in Lyon, but it was transferred to Paris in 1889. Nearly every form of Asian art is represented in this enormous collection of works from all countries and periods: Cambodia, Vietnam, Korea, China, Nepal, Afghanistan… a true voyage! And to finish, there's a little *salon de thé* nearby where you can enjoy Asian cuisine.

6 Pl. d'Iéna, 16e. 01 56 52 53 00.
www.guimet.fr – Admission fee.

V No. 16-07 (4 Rue de Longchamp, 16e).

Taking a Break

BAR DES THÉÂTRES

Nonchalantly sip a diabolo-grenadine at the bar of this legendary but friendly café, where it's not uncommon to find yourself sharing a barquette with a superstar of the cinema or theatre.

☕ 44 Rue Jean-Goujon, 8e. 01 47 23 34 63.
www.bardestheatres.fr
Open daily, 6am–2am.

V No. 08-45 (3 Av. Montaigne, 8e).

PLAZA ATHÉNÉE

The bar of the Plaza Athénée has managed to marry the modernity of a bright bar, with hypnotic blue notes, and the old wood panelling of this legendary hotel. Your order is taken on an iPad, which is a bit gimmicky, but the cocktails are delicious. People come here to see and be seen, and you need to be able to find a place between the Louboutin-heeled jet-set and jet-lagged Japanese tourists.

🍸 25 Av. Montaigne, 8e. 01 53 67 66 65.
www.plaza-athenee-paris.fr – Open daily, 6pm–2am.

V No. 08-45 (3 Av. Montaigne, 8e).

CHEZ FRANCIS

Welcome chez Francis: a luxurious, typically Parisian brasserie with a focus on comfort, which offers a stunning view of the Eiffel Tower. After having enjoyed traditional roast beef from Normandy or roast leg of lamb, you're only a few pedal strokes away from the Musée d'Art Moderne de la Ville de Paris.

🍽 7 Pl. de l'Alma, 8e. 01 47 20 86 83. Open daily, noon–midnight – www.chezfrancis-restaurant.com

V No. 08-45 (3 Av. Montaigne, 8e).

CRAZY HORSE

Good Champagne and vibrant paintings shape the place. The audience willingly let themselves be bewitched by the girls of the Crazy Horse and by the rather crazy atmosphere of this almost mythic Parisian cabaret.

🎭 12 Av. George-V, 8e. 01 47 23 32 32.
www.lecrazyhorseparis.com

V No. 08-45 (3 Av. Montaigne, 8e).

Calendar of Events
The exhibitions at the Palais de Tokyo, the Musée d'Art Moderne and the Musée Galliera
http://blog.velib.paris.fr/en/?s=musees16eEN

⭐ A Word From Vélib'

The Grail is at the end of this last stage, and it will have been worth it! Get ready for a slightly uphill ride along Avenue du Président-Wilson to the Trocadéro. If it's too steep, stop half way and take advantage of one of the avenue's museums.

Musée d'Art Moderne

MAM is housed in the former Pavillon de l'Électricité from the World Fair of 1937. And, appropriately enough, you can see here one of the largest paintings in the world: *La Fée Électricité* by Raoul Dufy (250 juxtaposed panels, totalling 600 m^2/6460 ft^2). The museum covers the great artistic movements of the 20th and 21st centuries (Fauvism, Cubism, Dadaïsm, Surrealism, etc.) with permanent collections and temporary exhibitions.

11 Av. du Président-Wilson, 16ᵉ. 01 53 67 40 00.
www.mam.paris.fr – Closed Mon.
🅥 No. 08-46 (2 Av. Marceau, 8ᵉ).

Palais de Tokyo

We mention the Palais de Toykyo because there's always something fun and at the forefront of hip and happening here. Open until midnight, it's the trendiest museum in the capital. This contemporary arts venue rotates its temporary exhibitions at the speed of lightning.

13 Av. du Président-Wilson, 16ᵉ. 01 81 97 35 88.
www.palaisdetokyo.com – Closed Tue.
🅥 No. 08-46 (2 Av. Marceau, 8ᵉ).

The terrace of the Musée d'Art Moderne

Place du Trocadéro

One of the best places to get beautiful views of Paris, and thus a haunt of photographers. From the central forecourt of the Palais de Chaillot, or the Esplanade des Droits-de-l'Homme, there's a splendid view over the Trocadéro gardens below, adorned with sculptures and fountains. The Seine is at your feet, flowing under the Pont d'Iéna, and then there's the Eiffel Tower, the Champ-de-Mars and the École Militaire. In the evening, the Trocadéro gardens benefit from spectacular lighting, like the Eiffel Tower, which sparkles at all hours, and the illuminations of the Champ-de-Mars.

🅥 nº16-14 (4 Av. d'Eylau, 16ᵉ).

Palais de Chaillot

The edifice was built for the World Fair of 1937 on the site of the former Palais du Trocadéro, whose old framework was kept by the architects for the new structure. It is composed of two large curved colonnaded wings separated by a central forecourt. The left wing houses the Théâtre National de Chaillot and the Cité de l'Architecture et du Patrimoine, which displays models of the architectural masterpieces from the 12th to 18th centuries. It also traces the evolution of urbanism from 1850 to the present day. In the right wing is the Musée de l'Homme and the Musée National de la Marine, which evokes the history of the French navy with some outstanding models. You can also see models of famous liners such as the *Titanic*, here.

1 Pl. du Trocadéro et du 11-Novembre, 16ᵉ.
01 58 51 52 00. www.citechaillot.fr/fr/musee/
🅥 nº16-14 (4 Av. d'Eylau, 16ᵉ).

Aquarium de Paris (Ciné-Aqua)

Want to see fish in the middle of Paris? The Aquarium de Paris (Ciné-Aqua), not far from the Trocadéro gardens, displays 500 aquatic species. There are also three cinemas, screening animations and marine documentaries. A pleasure for old and young alike.

5 Av. Albert-de-Mun, 16ᵉ.
01 40 69 23 23. www.cineaqua.com
🅥 nº16-14 (4 Av. d'Eylau, 16ᵉ).

Taking a Break

FROG XVI
The Frog has found its niche in creating a relaxed, very British atmosphere in an English pub serving classic British dishes as well as more international ones. People of all ages come here and the beer is chilled. This very convivial place also screens live sports matches.

🍸 110 Av. Kléber, 16ᵉ. 01 47 27 88 88.
www.frogpubs.com – Open daily, noon–2am.
✅ No. 16-14 (4 Av. d'Eylau, 16ᵉ).

TOKYO EAT
Be warned: they don't serve sushi or yakitori here; it's not a Japanese restaurant but rather a modern brasserie: free-range chicken curry wrapped in a banana leaf, *confit of aubergine* with a peanut sauce and the unmissable *yuzu* in a creamy sauce on a virgin *baba*. The cuisine is modern like the neighbouring museum. A total change of scene for your palate!

🍽 13 Av. du Président-Wilson, 16ᵉ. 01 47 20 00 29. Closed Tue.
✅ No. 16-07 (4 Rue de Longchamp, 16ᵉ).

CARETTE
Carette is a *maison de pâtisserie* founded in 1927, which sets the scene here. This is a lovely place in which to relax and enjoy a *macaron* or the wonderful pastries on the menu, making the most of a moment of exquisite self-indulgence. A perfect place, in fact, in which to celebrate the end of your bike trip across Paris.

🍴 4 Pl. du Trocadéro, 16ᵉ. 01 47 27 98 85.
www.carette-paris.com – Open daily, 7am–11:30pm.
✅ No. 16-14 (4 Av. d'Eylau, 16ᵉ).

BERT'S ALMA-MARCEAU
If you fancy a cup of coffee in a modern, elegant setting, then head to Bert's. You're served quickly and the food is pretty good. From its sandwiches to its breakfast menus and salads, there's bound to be something that will delight you.

🍴 4 Av. du Président-Wilson, Paris 8ᵉ. 01 47 23 48 37.
www.berts.fr – Open daily, 8am–8:30pm.
✅ No. 08-46 (2 Av. Marceau, 8ᵉ).

LE BARON
Le Baron isn't open to everyone and can be a bit elitist. But the reason it's one of the most popular clubs in Paris is that it has that touch of eccentricity that's peculiar to Parisian nightlife. We've even bumped into Björk and Sofia Coppola here!

🍴 6 Av. Marceau, Paris 8ᵉ. 01 47 20 04 01.
Open daily, 11pm–5am.
✅ No. 08-46 (2 Av. Marceau, 8ᵉ).

SCHWARTZ'S DELI
Meals are served quickly without this being "fast food". Schwartz's Deli is a mix of Jewish deli dishes and typical New York fare. People flock here for lunch and you'll need to be patient to get a place to eat.

🍽 7 Av. d'Eylau, 16ᵉ. 01 47 04 73 61.
www.schwartzsdeli.fr – Closed Thu.
✅ No. 16-14 (4 Av. d'Eylau, 16ᵉ).

51

ALMA MARKET
Stalls displaying fresh fruit, colourful vegetables, large hams, and tasty cheeses: welcome to the Alma market! You'll enjoy strolling around to find the dish you most fancy among the specialties from around the world. An ideal place to stock up on provisions for a picnic at the Trocadéro.

🍴 11-13 Av. du Président-Wilson, 16ᵉ. Open Wed and Sat.
✅ No. 08-46 (2 Av. Marceau, 8ᵉ).

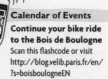

Calendar of Events
Continue your bike ride to the Bois de Boulogne
Scan this flashcode or visit http://blog.velib.paris.fr/en/?s=boisboulogneEN

Route 3 *From Luxurious to Bohemian Paris*

From the Place Charles-de-Gaulle – the hub of Paris in the centre of which proudly stands the Arc de Triomphe – to the Parc Monceau, this route though chic neighbourhoods follows tree-lined avenues that are dotted with luxury boutiques. Continue pedalling for a while after Villiers and you'll suddenly find yourself in Pigalle, the heart of raunchy Paris, which blithely taunts the imposing basilica of Sacré-Cœur standing at the top of the Butte Montmartre. Here bars and cabarets await you in the winding alleys of a very different Paris.

....

STAGE 1 ÉTOILE TO PLACE DES TERNES

✪ A Word From Vélib' ....

There are lots of stations around the Arc de Triomphe. As you're higher up here, the number of bikes available may be limited, however. Check using the Vélib' app or on the terminal screens. Before you set off, check the brakes, as on the first stage of the route you'll be coasting downhill! Go down Avenue de Wagram to Place des Ternes then turn right onto Boulevard de Courcelles. After a few blocks, there's a lovely path to follow.

Place de l'Étoile

This is without doubt the most well-known roundabout in Paris for motorists, who have to forge a path around it, with 12 avenues converging here, including the "*voie triomphale*", the Champs-Élysées. Once the promenade of high society, today it's the international showcase of modernity and luxury, dominated by the Arc de Triomphe. Previously known as the Place de l'Étoile (the name by which it still often goes), it was renamed Place Charles-de-Gaulle in 1970, four days after the general's death. It's not certain that he would have appreciated the honour, however, as he believed that the Unknown Soldier should have been buried in a place with no other connotation.

🅥 No. 08-28 (1 Rue Arsène-Houssaye, 8ᵉ).

Arc de Triomphe

Fifty metres (164 ft) tall and 45 m (148 ft) wide, the Arc de Triomphe was built between 1806 and 1836, to celebrate the glory of Napoleon's Grande Armée. Beneath it is the Tomb of the Unknown Soldier, to which the president of the Republic pays tribute each year during the July 14 procession. Take a deep breath, then climb its 284 steps to reach the top, from where you can admire the view and the perfect alignment of the Champs-Élysées with prestigious monuments such as the obelisk of the Place de la Concorde, the Arc du Carrousel, the Pyramid of the Louvre (and, in season, the big wheel of the Jardin des Tuileries). On the opposite side stands the Grande Arche de La Défense.

The lights of the Arc de Triomphe

ON THE ITINERARY

A ride through chic neighbourhoods, from the Place Charles-de-Gaulle, via Batignolles to the unmissable Moulin Rouge and the shady Paris of Pigalle.

Departure Point:
Étoile (No. 02-28 – 1 Rue Arsène-Houssaye, 8ᵉ)
Arrival Point:
Pigalle (No. 09-05 – Square d'Anvers, 9ᵉ)

53

Place de l'Étoile, 8ᵉ. 01 55 37 73 77. Open 10am–10:30pm. www.arc-de-triomphe.monuments-nationaux.fr
No. 08-28 (1 Rue Arsène-Houssaye, 8ᵉ).

Place des Ternes

Following Avenue Wagram, coast down to Place des Ternes, where you can admire one of the famous *édicules*, metro entrances designed by the architect Hector Guimard (1867–1942), a leading representative of Art Nouveau. As you continue your route along the Boulevard de Courcelles, cast a glance down the first road on your right.
You will see the unusual Cathédrale Saint-Alexandre-Nevski, Paris's Byzantine-Russian-style orthodox church, built between 1859 and 1861. It is distinguished by its architectural originality (it has recently been restored): five pyramids topped with onion domes, as well as frescos, gilding, and icons embellishing a Greek cross. You could almost forget you're in Paris! On July 12, 1918, Pablo Picasso married Olga Khoklova here, with Max Jacob, Jean Cocteau, Guillaume Apollinaire, and Serge Diaghilev as witnesses.

No. 17-45 (5 Pl. des Ternes, 8ᵉ).

Musée Jacquemart-André

You will find the museum near the intersection of Rue de Courcelles and Boulevard Haussmann. This splendid mansion belonged to a pair of collectors, Nélie and Édouard André, who were avid connoisseurs of 18th century art. They travelled throughout Europe and the Far East in search of rare works, and commissioned the architect Henri Parent to build this palace to house their artwork, furniture, and other artifacts.

158 Bd. Haussmann, 8ᵉ. 01 45 62 11 59.
www.musee-jacquemart-andre.com
Open daily, 10am–9pm (Sun 6pm)
No. 08-34 (49 Rue de Berri, 8ᵉ).

- Parc Monceau
- Musée Nissim-de-Camondo
- Musée Cernuschi
- Musée Jean-Jacques Henner

- Neva Cuisine
- Marché de la Rue de Lévis
- Aux Merveilleux de Fred

STAGES 2-3

- Place Charles-de-Gaulle
- Arc de Triomphe
- Place des Ternes
- Musée Jacquemart-André

- Le Comptoir de l'Arc
- Le Balzac
- Chez Raspoutine
- Le Lido
- Publicis Drugstore
- Louis Vuitton
- Delitaly
- Mariage Frères

STAGE 1

BD PEREIRE

WAGRAM

17-20
17-21
17-119

BD MALESHERBES
RUE CARDINET
RUE DE TOCQUEV

MALESHERBES

MUSÉE
J.-J. HENNER

17-19

17-26

RUE DE PRONY

MONCEAU
17-18

BD DE COURCE

RUE LAUGIER

RUE DE COURCELLES

17-25

2

MUSÉE NISSIM-
DE-CAMONDO
CER

AV. NIEL

17-45   08-55

PLACE
DES TERNES

COURCELLES

PARC
MONCEAU

08-44

RUE DE LI

AV. DE WAGRAM

TERNES

RUE DU FG-SAINT-HONORÉ

RUE DE MONCEAU

08-36

AV. MAC-MAHON

17-46

17-34

MUSÉE
JACQUEMART-ANDRÉ

AV. HOCHE

08-54

08-43

BD HAUSSMAN

CHARLES DE GAULLE
ÉTOILE
17-33

08-34

1

08-57

08-56

AV. DE FRIEDLAND

ARC DE
TRIOMPHE

08-28

08-102

08-103

16-07

PLACE-
CHARLES-
DE-GAULE

ST-PHILIPPE
DU ROULE

08-52

AV. DES CHAMPS-ÉLYSÉES

KLÉBER

GEORGE V

LAMARCK CAULAINCOURT
RUE CAULAINCOURT
18-16
18-15
18-13
CHÂTEAU ROUGE
ESPACE DALÍ
SACRÉ COEUR
18-02
BD BARBÈS
18-07
BARBÈS ROCHECHOUART
BD DE LA CHAPELLE
18-04
18-06
18-05
ABBESSES
DES SES
ANVERS
LE LOUXOR
10-41
PIGALLE
BD DE RO
6
18-41
09-03
09-05
CHY
5
BD MAGENTA
09-06
10-107
09-17
RUE DES MARTYRS
RUE DE CLIGNANCOURT
RUE DE ROCHECHOUART
10-33
GARE DU NORD
09-07
RUE DE DUNKERQUE
9-20
09-08
10-53
GEORGES
RUE DE MAUBEUGE
09-16
09-108
16-07
09-15
09-09
RUE LA FAYETTE
POISSONNIÈRE
CADET
NOTRE DAME E LORETTE
LE PELETIER
09-101
09-113
RUE DU FG-POISSONNIÈRE
RUE

- Butte Montmartre
- Basilique du Sacré-Cœur
- Vineyards of Montmartre
- "Bohemian" Cabarets
- Espace Dali
- The Louxor

- Les Deux Moulins
- La Halle Saint Pierre
- Au RendezVous des Amis
- Le Floors
- Yoom
- Studio 28
- Autour de Midi... et Minuit
- Guerrisol
- Mamie Blue
- Galerie 9e Art

STAGE 6

STAGE 5

Taking a Break

CINÉMA LE BALZAC

This neighbourhood theatre has always been a staunch defender of arthouse films in Paris. They are continually seeking to introduce audiences to new and current directors. And beyond traditional screenings, Le Balzac has made a name for itself with films that are rarely seen elsewhere.

1 Rue Balzac, 8ᵉ. 01 45 61 10 60. www.cinemabalzac.com
No. 08-52 (2 Rue Balzac, 8ᵉ).

PUBLICIS DRUGSTORE

A disciple of chef Alain Ducasse directs brunch here. Just watch all the mini plates and verrines emerge, carrying coleslaw, smoked salmon and soft boiled eggs in every way imaginable. Then, prepare for the cakes and pastries, like Black Forest gateau and luscious strawberry tarts. The Drugstore and the gourmet food shop are alo the perfect place to find a gift.

133 Av. des Champs-Élysées, 8ᵉ. 01 44 43 75 07.
www.publicisdrugstore.com
Open daily until 2am.
No. 08-28 (1 Rue Arsène-Houssaye, 8ᵉ).

CHEZ RASPOUTINE

In this old Russian cabaret near the Champs-Élysées, admire the sculptures on the ceiling, the thick-pile carpet and the red banquettes. Everything's here to ensure enchanting evenings that last until dawn. The bar is unique, and its always full of atmosphere.

58 Rue de Bassano, 8ᵉ. 01 47 20 02 90.
www.raspoutine.org – Open Thu–Sat, 11:30pm–6am.
No. 81-15 (10 Rue Vernet, 8ᵉ).

MARIAGE FRÈRES

The famous Mariage Frères teahouse is one of our favourite places in Paris. You can buy boxes of loose tea, but you should really visit the adjoining salon de thé with its period decor and delicious, fresh cakes and pastries. You could stay here for hours, but it's important to learn to share and to leave your place free so that everyone can enjoy this very special place !

260 Rue du Fbg.-Saint-Honoré, 8ᵉ. 01 46 22 18 54.
www.mariagefreres.com
Open daily, 10:30am–7:30pm.
No. 08-55 (87 Bd. de Courcelles, 8ᵉ).

COMPTOIR DE L'ARC

Large picture windows let the light shine in on the pink and wood furnishings of the Comptoir de l'Arc. The food here is French and the prices very reasonable: count on paying €6 for a cocktail. It's one of the best value for money restaurants in the area and you eat well … Tuck in!

73 Av. Marceau, 16ᵉ. 01 47 20 72 04.
Open Mon–Fri, 7am–midnight
No. 08-03 (63 Rue Galilée, 8ᵉ).

LOUIS VUITTON

The emblem of luxury in Paris, Louis Vuitton has showcased French savoir-faire worldwide. The flagship of the monogrammed brand is an essential place to stop and shop on the world's most beautiful avenue. The store is often packed but always ready to welcome you. We recommend a visit to the top floor, which is devoted to beautiful and free exhibitions.

101 Av. des Champs-Élysées, 8ᵉ. 01 53 57 52 00.
www.louisvuitton.fr
Open Mon–Sat, 10am–8pm; Sun 11am–7pm.
No. 81-15 (10 Rue Vernet, 8ᵉ).

LIDO

This cabaret on the Champs-Élysées always know how to charm visitors from around the world. Its Belle Époque interior lets you get whisked away by the wild dancing of its topless dancers. Open 365 days a year, it's one of chic, glamorous Paris's great venues.

116 Bis Av. des Champs-Élysées, 8ᵉ. 01 40 76 56 10.
www.lido.fr – No. 81-15 (10 Rue Vernet, 8ᵉ).

DELITALY

An Italian deli that smells wonderfully of pesto and pasta, and serves daily specials and a varied menu filled with fresh produce. It's a rather noisy and always lively place, though, so we wouldn't recommend it for an intimate tête-à-tête.

21 Rue Poncelet, 17ᵉ. 01 42 27 52 19.
www.delitaly.fr – Open daily, 10am–8:30pm.
No. 17-45 (5 Pl. des Ternes, 17ᵉ).

57

⊛ A Word From Vélib'

Stop in front of the railings of the Parc Monceau to recover from the pseudo flat path you've just cycled up. If the weather is nice, you can even have a little nap on the park's lawn. Then set off again in the direction of Place de Clichy. Keep going straight ahead on the Boulevard de Courcelles, then on the Boulevard des Batignolles. From Villiers, take the bike path along the middle strip, under the shade of the trees.

Parc Monceau

This park originally belonged to the Duke of Chartres. In 1779, he asked the painter and landscape architect Carmontelle (1717–1806) to create for him a half-German, half-English garden, a sort of "land of illusions". It would include a pagoda, Dutch windmills, a Swiss farm, feudal ruins, a Roman temple, a pyramid, and an oval pond surrounded by Corinthian columns and white statues. Lining the paths, you encounter varied species of trees: Oriental plane, sycamore maple, and Ginkgo biloba. It's both an exotic and idyllic walk – in the middle of Paris!

✔ No. 17-18 (4 Rue Thann, 17ᵉ).

Musée Nissim-de-Camondo

You need to imagine, during the Second Empire, two brothers, Abraham Behor and Nissim, Jewish bankers from Constantinople. Here they are, building two mansions on the edge of Parc Monceau. Later, Count Moïse de Camondo inherits the mansion from his father,

Nissim. He has it razed then rebuilt, between 1911 and 1914, taking his inspiration from the Petit Trianon, with the intention of housing his collection of works of art in a setting that evokes classical art as well as the Belle Époque. His grandson bequeathed everything to the Musée des Arts Décoratifs, and the Musée Nissim-de-Camondo was opened in 1936. The last heirs of this family died in Auschwitz in 1945.

63 Rue de Monceau, 8ᵉ. 01 53 89 06 40.
Open Wed–Sun, 10am–5:30pm.
✔ No. 08-36 (39 Rue de Lisbonne, 8ᵉ).

Musée Cernuschi

Right nearby, the Musée Cernuschi, one of the oldest museums in Paris, specializes in Asian art: China, Japan, Vietnam, Korea. Numerous pieces retrace the history of Chinese civilization, from prehistory to the 13th century, but you can also see interesting temporary exhibits here. We owe all this to a banker of Italian origin, Henri Cernuschi. Fleeing to France in 1850, he travelled with an art critic friend and acquired, in two years, more than 5000 works of art, notably bronzes. He set up a room in his mansion on Avenue Velázquez to show off the highlight of his collection, the 4.4 m (14.5 ft) tall Buddha Amida, which you can still admire in the museum.

7 Av. Velázquez, 8ᵉ. 01 53 96 21 50.
www.cernuschi.paris.fr
Open Tue–Sun, 10am–6pm.
✔ No. 08-37 (75 Rue de Monceau, 8ᵉ).

Parc Monceau

Musée Cernuschi

Musée Jean-Jacques Henner

On the other side of the Boulevard de Courcelles, heading north, you will find the Musée Jean-Jacques Henner. Housed in a very fine 19th century mansion that has recently been restored (2008–2009), with an interior that is both peaceful and eclectic, this museum is worth a detour. You can see here more than 500 works by the painter Jean-Jacques Henner (1829–1905), who is said to have adored redheads! A portrait and landscape painter who was influenced by Symbolism, he was popular for his nymphs and female nudes.

His collections retrace his artistic career, which began in his native Alsace and took him to Paris, where he made a name for himself, via the Villa Médicis, where he stayed after having won the Prix de Rome. In particular, you can admire a large number of the works from his studio and gain an understanding of how an "official" painter worked during the Impressionist period.

43 Av. de Villiers, 17ᵉ. 01 47 63 42 73.
www.musee-henner.fr – Open Wed–Mon, 11am–6pm.
🅥 No. 17-19 (20 Rue de Phalsbourg, 17ᵉ).

Taking a Break

RUE DE LÉVIS MARKET

After the last museum, you're not far from the Rue de Lévis market, between Rue Cardinet and Rue Legendre. Go and have a wander along this little pedestrian street and explore its permanent market of fruit, vegetables, and flowers alongside other traders with very appetizing stalls!
No. 17-24 (1 Pl. Prosper-Goubaux, 17ᵉ).

AUX MERVEILLEUX DE FRED

Love at first sight doesn't exist solely in terms of romance: a pâtisserie, too, can have the same effect on you! The *merveilleux* sold here are a real treat. Foodies, we have only three words to say to you: go for it!
7 Rue de Tocqueville, 17ᵉ. 01 42 27 86 63. Open Mon–Fri, 12:30–2pm and 7–10:30pm – www.auxmerveilleux.com .
🅥 No. 17-48 (12 Rue de Tocqueville, 17ᵉ).

NEVA CUISINE

If you're not yet familiar with the concept of bistronomy, the contraction of "gastronomy" and "bistro", you need to discover it here – a real dining experience that will tantalize your taste buds. Count on paying around €30 for a set menu of starter and main course or main course and dessert.
2 Rue de Berne, 8ᵉ. 01 45 22 18 91.
Open Mon–Fri, 12:30–2pm and 7–10:30pm.
🅥 No. 08-11 (1 Rue Clapeyron, 8ᵉ).

✹ A Word From Vélib'

Leave your Vélib' at a station to visit the Batignolles district in the north of Paris on foot. Then set off again on your bike, following the Boulevard de Clichy, which is on your right a few metres further on. From there, rejoin the central path and continue on to Pigalle.

Batignolles

A former hamlet of Paris, which today has a very Parisian atmosphere that is a mixture of Bohemian exuberance and middle-class discretion. Stroll along Rue des Dames, then Rue Legendre or Rue Cardinet and the Square des Batignolles. Useful to know: the Square des Batignolles is spared the fate of the capital's other parks and gardens, which become invaded by Parisians in need of some fresh air; it's therefore the perfect place to linger for a nap in the shade. Enjoy roaming around this gently rolling English-style garden, with its very exotic vegetation, river miniature lake, and grotto. (The park was designed by Baron Haussmann, nostalgic for a trip to England.) There are also ducks, little bridges, and the fake rocks overgrown with ivy and moss.

🆅 No. 17-13 (62 Rue Legendre, 17ᵉ).

Église Saint-Michel

Unusual! Take the Passage Saint-Michel, situated on Avenue de Saint-Ouen after La Fourche. At the end is the red bell-tower of the Église Saint-Michel. This early 20th-century church, a mixture of Byzantine and futurist styles, is attached at the rear to the former building, whose entrance is on Avenue de Saint-Ouen.

3 Pl. Saint-Jean, 17ᵉ. 01 43 87 33 94.
www.saintmichel-paris.fr
Open Tue–Sat, 7:30am–noon and 2–7pm.
🆅 No. 17-02 (4 Rue de la Condamine, 17ᵉ).

Place de Clichy

In the centre of the square, which is very popular with Parisians, is a statue of Maréchal Moncey (1754–1842). Standing 8 m (26 ft) tall, it recalls the bravery of the man in charge of the National Guard in late 1814 during the time of Napoleon's defeat. With his men, he fought against troops of Cossack soldiers, led by the "traitor" Langeron, on the Clichy barrier. This square, which had been marked out by Ledoux, served as a border for excise duty. Today, it's one of the city's hubs, linking the chic districts of Batignolles and the Carrefour de l'Europe to the "rougher", more Bohemian ones of Pigalle and Montmartre.

🆅 No. 08-12 (10 Bd. des Batignolles, 8ᵉ).

Musée Gustave-Moreau

More than 15,000 paintings, drawings, illustrated books, and, in short, everything that served as a source of inspiration to the famous symbolist painter Gustave Moreau (1826–1898) is exhibited here! As had been his wish during his lifetime, you'll also find his own works here in his old family home. Part of the space is called, rather movingly, "le petit musée sentimental" and displays his furniture and personal mementos. Lovers of period interiors will be delighted.

14 Rue de La-Rochefoucauld, 9ᵉ. 01 48 74 38 50.
www.musee-moreau.fr
Open daily, Wed–Mon 10am–12:45pm and 2–7:15pm.
🆅 No. 09-26 (28 Rue Jean-Baptiste-Pigalle, 9ᵉ).

Musée de la Vie Romantique

Tucked away at the end of a cul-de-sac, this museum is housed in the former home of the painter Ary Scheffer (1795–1858). It's a real haven of peace in which are exhibited souvenirs belonging to him and his friend George Sand. On sunny days, enjoy the beautiful flower garden and the tearoom in the glasshouse.

16 Rue Chaptal, 9ᵉ. 01 55 31 95 67.
www.vie-romantique.paris.fr – Open Tue–Sun, 10am-6pm.
Ⓥ No. 09-27 (24 Rue de Douai, 9ᵉ).

Moulin Rouge

This is without question the most famous cabaret in Paris! The Moulin Rouge has existed in the pleasure district since 1889. Parisians coming here for the first time often regret having wrongfully assumed that this venue was just for tourists. In the basement, as an extra, the cabaret hides the Machine du Moulin Rouge, a big nightclub where you can dance the night away. Events are varied, from live concerts to DJ nights.

82 Bd. de Clichy, 18ᵉ. 01 53 09 82 82. www.moulinrouge.fr
Ⓥ No. 18-43 (55 Bd. de Clichy, 18ᵉ).

Place Blanche

This square takes its name from Rue Blanche, which was so called because of the whiteness of the nearby gypsum quarries of Montmartre. The cars and carts that carried their loads down this road used to leave traces of it behind them and all the houses were covered in white plaster.

Ⓥ No. 09-38 (50 Bis Rue de Douai, 9ᵉ).

Place Saint-Georges

In the centre of this little Neo-Classical-style square stands a fountain that in former times was used for watering thirsty horses. Today it is surmounted by a fine bust of the artist Gavarni. On its base is a relief depicting a scene from the Paris Carnival. This place – the heart of Nouvelle Athènes (New Athens), so called in reference to the area's profusion of Doric columns and other arches – was in past times the haunt of the Romantics: lovers Sand and Chopin would meet up with Bizet on the Square d'Orléans. At no. 27 stands the Hôtel Thiers, where the politician Adolphe Thiers was arrested during Napoléon III's coup in 1851. Truffaut filmed *Le Dernier Métro* not far from here, in the theatre at the top of Rue Saint-Georges.

Ⓥ No. 09-21 (56 Rue Saint-Georges, 9ᵉ).

61

The Moulin Rouge

 ALSO WORTH SEEING ON THE WAY

MUSÉE DE L'ÉROTISME ★ ★ ★
CITÉ MALESHERBES ★ ★
PLACE ESTIENNE-D'ORVES ★ ★
ÉGLISE DE LA TRINITÉ ★ ★ ★

CINÉMA DES CINÉASTES

"Le Cinéma par ceux qui le font" ("Films by those who make them.") The tone is set! This cinema focuses exclusively on arthouse films, giving priority to foreign films and seeking to introduce film genres that generally receive little exposure, such as short films and documentaries.

🎦 7 Av. de Clichy, 17ᵉ. 01 53 42 40 20.
www.cinema-des-cineastes.fr
🚇 No. 17-14 (12 Av. de Clichy, 17ᵉ).

LE BISTROT DES CINÉASTES

A red-brick interior and resolutely film-based dishes: *Festen* (a Scandinavian film, so smoked salmon, blinis, and crème fraîche); *Un chien andalou* (Spanish cooked meats); *Delicatessen* (pastrami and bagel) or *La Belle Verte* (salad), and, for dessert *Rue des Plaisirs*. The focus is on quality produce: smoked fish from Olsen, cheese from Aléosse, wine from Bourgogne…

🍸 7 Av. de Clichy, 17ᵉ. 01 53 42 40 34.
Open daily, 6pm–midnight.
🚇 No. 17-14 (12 Av. de Clichy, 17ᵉ).

WEST BAR

Open the doors into this bar and you'll find you've been teleported to the Wild West of the 19th century. The ambience is that of a saloon, with subdued lighting and red-velvet armchairs. The owner will greet you dressed as a cowboy, and a few regulars leaning on the bar also look as though they've come straight out of a Western. A small electric train runs on the ceiling, and screens show episodes of *The Wild Wild West*, an American cult TV series of the 1960s. Set off in conquest of the Wild West!

🍸 61 Rue Legendre, 17ᵉ. 01 46 27 31 59.
🚇 No. 17-13 (62 Rue Legendre, 17ᵉ).

INSTITUT VATEL

Institut Vatel trains the top chefs of the future. Come and enjoy a menu worthy of a Michelin-starred restaurant for €33, made up of seasonal dishes that are sophisticated and harmonious from start to finish. Just wait until you see the dessert trolley! As a plus, no one will mind if you get out your camera to photograph one of these caramelized or chocolate works of art!

🍽 122 Rue Nollet, 17ᵉ. 01 42 26 26 60.
www.vatel.fr –Open Mon–Fri.
🚇 No. 17-111 (109 Rue Lemercier, 17ᵉ).

LE CLUB DES CINQ

When a group of friends launch into the traditional cuisine of French childhoods, the results are sing with flavour! Everything here is so delicious that you're likely to rave over practically every mouthful. The shelves are stacked with classic children's books and toys, while the walls are covered with characters from comics and other heroes from the 1980s.

🍽 57 Rue des Batignolles, 17ᵉ. 01 53 04 94 73.
www.leclubdes5.fr
Open daily, evenings only on Mon and Sat.
🚇 No. 17-13 (62 Rue Legendre, 17ᵉ).

LE DIAPASON
The secret's got out on this restaurant over the last few years, which means that it's now difficult to reserve a table. The view will reveal the whole of Paris to you. The Eiffel Tower looks close at hand, while Julien Roucheteau's cooking takes the road south with lamb chops with sage and regular deliveries of fish.

12-14 Rue Joseph-de-Maistre, 18ᵉ. 01 44 92 34 00. www.terrass-hotel.com

No. 18-03 (2 Rue Joseph-de-Maistre, 18ᵉ).

DELIZIE
For a little detour to Sicily, make Delizie your next stop! Here you'll find *buffitieri, sfincione, arancini…* And if you don't know what they are, now is your chance to discover this gastronomy. Antipasti and pasta are also highlighted, as are the delicious homemade sauces.

15 Rue Damrémont, 18ᵉ. 09 81 88 45 39. www.deliziesiciliane-paris.com
Open daily, 10:30am–10:30pm.

No. 18-01 (6 Rue Damrémont, 18ᵉ).

BISTROT DES DAMES
A staircase leads down to a lovely shaded courtyard in front of a small hotel with retro charm. There are a few tables under the trees, a little path, and Chinese lanterns hanging from the branches. Enjoy Mariage Frères tea or fresh ginger juice here.

18 Rue des Dames, 17ᵉ. 01 45 22 13 42.
Open daily, 12:30pm–2am.

No. 18-45 (2 Rue Pierre-Ginier, 17ᵉ).

GROOVE STORE
The place to go if you're a fan of Black music, though there's also a lot of other staff on offer. Groove Store is loved for its prices, which are much better than anything you'll find on the Internet.

29 Rue des Dames, 17ᵉ. 01 44 90 09 46.
www.groove-store.com – Open Tue–Sat, 3–7:30pm.

No. 17-12 (16 Rue des Batignolles, 17ᵉ).

BULLES EN TÊTE
At this bookstore, they use a fine-tooth comb to try to unearth graphic novels and comics that have yet to be properly acknowledged. One distinctive feature of the store is its impressive manga collection of all genres.

54 Rue des Dames, 17ᵉ. 09 53 31 12 92.
Open Mon–Sat, 10:30am–8pm.

No. 17-12 (16 Rue des Batignolles, 17ᵉ).

63

🌸 A Word From Vélib'

You've arrived in the heart of Pigalle, and the Sacré-Cœur is very close! Continue your ride along the bike path of the roads middle strip, passing the red neon signs of cabarets and sex shops. You'll soon come to the Anvers metro station, the arrival point of this route.

Place Pigalle

Today, Pigalle is known throughout the world as a pleasure and entertainment district; but Place Pigalle draws its name from an 18th-century sculptor whose studio was located in an adjacent road. It should be said that Pigalle has also been linked with marginality, slums, and crime: around the 1930s, the area was synonymous with the underworld, drugs, and thugs (with whom writers like Aragon and Céline freely associated). And to think that Pigalle had initially an aristocratic *quartier*, like Nouvelle Athènes, bringing together the chic and the artistic life! The "mafia" began to move out of the area only after the 1950s. During the second half of the 20th century, Place Pigalle became more touristy and had a facelift with the arrival of trendy cafés and concert halls.

🅥 No. 09-18 (1 Rue Duperre, 9e).

Place des Abbesses

This square owes its name to the Benedictine convent of Montmartre. During the Siege of Paris between 1588 and 1594, the "Vert Galant" (Henri IV) is said to have seduced the Mother Superior here, thus setting the example for the other nuns and his lieutenants. The lovestruck abesse allegedly followed Henri IV as far as Senlis, where she introduced him to a pretty cousin, Gabrielle d'Estrées; he then went off with her instead and she became his favourite! Could it be for these old romantic reasons that, right nearby, the "I love you" wall, which has become a mecca for lovers, was set up (2000) on Square Jehan-Rictus? Frédéric Baron collected more than 1500 declarations of love in Paris, in all languages. There are now 311 "I love you" on the wall, written in 280 languages and transcribed by calligrapher Claire Kito.

🅥 No. 18-04 (2 Pl. des Abbesses, 18e).

Place Émile-Goudeau and the Bateau-Lavoir

Place Émile-Goudeau is the most representative of artists thanks to the Bateau-Lavoir, a former piano factory that became a meeting place for artists at the end of the 19th century. Picasso, Braque, and Juan Gris, the creators of Cubism, as well as the writers Max Jacob, Apollinaire, and Marc Orlan used to meet here in rather precarious conditions. The house has also been occupied by Modigliani, Kees Van Dongen, and Brancusi. It was Max Jacob who gave it the name of *"bateau-lavoir"* (washing boat), because he used to say that the place was like a paint-splashed boat that was in need of a clean! The building was destroyed by a fire in 1970 but was subsequently rebuilt. Today, it provides studio and living spaces for artists. It is not open to the public.

🅥 No. 18-04 (2 Pl. des Abbesses, 18e).

Montmartre Cemetery

Construction of the 11 ha (27 acre) cemetery, in which maples watch over the dead, was completed in 1825. On a walk around the cemetery, you can visit 20,000 tombs, some of them belonging to people who have left their mark on France and its culture, including Goncourt, Renan, Stendhal, Zola, Degas, Berlioz, Berger, Guitry, and Dalida.

Open 9am–5:30pm.
🅥 No. 18-03 (2 Rue Joseph-de-Maistre, 18e).

ALSO WORTH SEEING ON THE WAY

VILLA LÉANDRE ★ ★ ★

The "I love you" wall (Square Jehan-Rictus)

Taking a Break

HÔTEL AMOUR

This little love nest helps couples rediscover one other. It's a place geared to lovers lacking intimacy or to those who are seeking thrills! The dishes served at the hotel's restaurant are good and simple, and you'll not find the bill too steep.

🍽 8 Rue de Navarin, 9ᵉ. 01 48 78 31 80. Open 8am–2am.
Ⓥ No. 09-20 (27 Rue Clauzel, 9ᵉ).

LE CARMEN

Settle into an armchair or on a Renaissance-style bed in this romantic salon with subdued lighting. Then sip a tailor-made cocktail in a private setting that is so intimate you'll have trouble leaving!

🍸 34 Rue Duperré, 9ᵉ. 01 45 25 50 00.
www.le-carmen.fr – Open daily, 10pm–5am.
Ⓥ No. 09-27 (24 Rue de Douai, 9ᵉ).

THE GLASS

The Glass team wanted to create a New York City feel in this cocktail bar, which is considered to be one of the best in Paris. The drinks menu offers an astonishing selection of beers as well as cocktails made with rare ingredients. Avoid weekends, when the small room is often packed.

🍸 7 Rue Frochot, 9ᵉ. Open daily, 7pm–2am.
Ⓥ No. 09-19 (38 Rue Victor-Massé, 9ᵉ).

LE VINGT HEURES VIN

The bar's distinctive decor makes you want to sit down with a glass of wine, a platter of cheese and charcuteries. The prices are affordable and the service invariably friendly.

🍸 17 Rue Joseph-de-Maistre, 18ᵉ. 09 54 66 50 67.
Closed Mon. Open evenings only.
Ⓥ No. 18-03 (2 Rue Joseph-de-Maistre, 18ᵉ).

Le Carmen

CHLOÉ. S

This "cupcakerie" is the epitome of American snack time: brightly coloured cupcakes and giant sprinkled whoopie pies will take you back to your childhood in two shakes of a sugar sprinkler. A real explosion of calories!

🍰 40 Rue Jean-Baptiste-Pigalle, 9ᵉ. 01 48 78 12 65.
www.cakechloes.com – Open Tue–Sun, 11am–7:30pm.
Ⓥ No. 09-26 (28 Rue Jean-Baptiste-Pigalle, 9ᵉ).

LA MAISON MÈRE

The new mecca of Parisian "bobocracy", La Maison Mère looks like a New York diner with its white tiles and bowler-hat-shaped pendant lights. You'll feel so at home here, you'll want to monopolize the bar all day and put the world to rights with the two owners.

🍽 4 Rue Navarin, 9ᵉ. 01 42 81 11 00.
www.lamaisonmere.fr – Open Mon–Sat, noon–3pm and 7pm–2am; Sun noon–4pm.
Ⓥ No. 09-20 (27 Rue Clauzel, 9ᵉ).

GALS ROCK

A shop dedicated to female rock culture. Here you'll find clothes, accessories, and CDs chosen by the managers. If you like the ambience, you can extend it by buying the compilation assembled by Clémence and Pauline.

🛍 17 Rue Henry-Monnier, 9ᵉ. 01 45 26 09 03.
www.galsrock.fr
Open Tue–Sat, noon–9pm; Sun, 10am–6pm.
Ⓥ No. 09-20 (27 Rue Clauzel, 9ᵉ).

LE BUS PALLADIUM

You may know this legendary rock venue, if only by name. It's impossible to miss it if you're wandering around the area after dark. So, go and move and groove – it'll do you good!

🎸 6 Rue Fontaine, 9ᵉ. 01 45 26 80 35.
www.lebuspalladium.com
Ⓥ No. 09-26 (28 Rue Jean-Baptiste-Pigalle, 9ᵉ).

65

Calendar of Events

Pigalle nightlife: What's on
Scan this flashcode or visit
http://blog.velib.paris.fr/en/
?s=pigallelanuitEN

❀ A Word From Vélib'

Montmartre is for elite Vélib' users. There are Vélib' stations at the foot of the hill where you can leave your bike: the climb up is challenging enough on foot to deter you from wanting to cycle up on your Vélib', and in any case, there isn't a station at the top! After your nice long ride, you'll be reassured to know that there's a funicular railway on the left of the hill to save you from having to walk up the 222 steps.

Butte Montmartre

The hill (*butte*) itself has the same character as the old villages of Montmartre, with its narrow steep streets that will charm and delight you as you stroll around. Climb up on foot or take the funicular railway (c. 130 m/426 ft elevation), opened in 1900, and relive scenes from the film *Amélie*! But from where did the hill get its name? During Gallo-Roman times, it was called the "Mont de Mars" because it was the site of a temple dedicated to the god of war. Before being annexed to Paris in 1860, Montmartre was an independent commune. At the end of the 17th century, this flourishing commune provided Paris with wheat, wine, and gypsum (plaster of Paris). As the popular French saying goes: "There's more of Montmartre in Paris than of Paris in Montmartre." The gypsum quarries closed in the 18th century. The production of wine ceased towards the end of the 19th century, although there remains a small square of vines that have been preserved for nostalgia's sake: the Clos de Montmartre. Every year, there's a celebration centred around the grape harvest. Between the 19th and 20th centuries, Montmartre welcomed some of the greatest French and foreign painters of the time, who had come to live in Paris: Pissarro, Toulouse-Lautrec, Van Gogh, Modigliani, Picasso... After the war, artists and writers chose to move toward Montparnasse and Saint-Germain.

Basilique du Sacré-Cœur

Just imagine that it was due to a law passed in 1873 by Catholic members of the National Assembly that the basilica was allowed to be built, through public subscription. Millions of French people contributed, often with modest sums. Architect Paul Abadie began the project in 1876. Completed just before the beginning of the First World War, the building was consacrated in 1919. Since then, it has become legendary, with its pristine cupolas, dome, and bell tower that can be seen from numerous points throughout Paris. The basilica is one of the most visited buildings in France, receiving 10 million visitors a year. An interesting fact: it preserves its beautiful white colour thanks to gypsum, which is "self-cleaning"when it rains!

35 Rue du Chevalier-de-la-Barre, 18ᵉ. 01 53 41 89 00. www.sacre-cœur-montmartre.com
Open daily, 6am–11:30pm.
Ⓥ No. 18-05; at the foot of the funicular (8 Rue Tardieu, 18ᵉ).

Vineyards of Montmartre

The Clos de Vigne de Montmartre, planted in 1933, stretches out over the slopes of the former Parc de la belle Gabrielle (where Gabrielle d'Estrées, a favourite of Henri IV's once lived). Much of

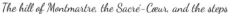

The hill of Montmartre, the Sacré-Cœur, and the steps

the hill was at one time covered with vineyards, and the winemakers pressed their grapes at the Convent des Abbesses. Would you like a little glass of Montmartre? In 1933, a plot planted with 1900 vines, 70 percent of them Gamay, was saved from urbanization. Its grapes are harvested annually and the few hundred bottles yielded are sold at the following year's harvest.

🆅 No. 18-17 (93 Rue Caulaincourt, 18ᵉ).

"Bohemian" Cabarets

On Rue Lepic, discover the old Moulin de la Galette, which in the 19th century hosted dances that were attended by Van Gogh, Utrillo, Toulouse-Lautrec, and Renoir. It is said that in 1814, during the Siege of Paris, the owner was nailed to the wings of his windmill and crushed; his widow collected his remins in a flour sack. It was his son who transformed the windmill into a dance hall in the 1860s. Between dances, *galettes* (pancakes) made with flour from the mill were served, hence the establishment's name. Opposite the vineyards is another famous cabaret, Au Lapin Agile, which has known different names: Au Rendez-Vous des Voleurs, Le Cabaret des Assassins, À Ma Campagne… In 1886, it was managed by Adèle Decerf whose speciality was stewed rabbit; around 1900, the illustrator André Gill designed the establishment's sign with a rabbit jumping from the pan; "le lapin à Gill" thus became Au Lapin Agile! In the early 20th century, singer-songwriter Aristide Bruant bought the cabaret and entrusted it to Frédéric Gérard, a charismatic character known as Père Frédé who was accompanied by his donkey, Lolo. The evenings he hosted here assembled the bohemians of Montmartre: Dorgelès, Renoir, Courteline, Picasso, Utrillo…

Espace Dalí

This former winery is the only permanent gallery in France that is entirely devoted to Salvador Dalí (1904–1989). It includes the largest collection in the world of sculptures and engravings by the master of Surrealism. Discover more than 300 works that have made the Catalan one of the major artists of the 20th century. The widow of the artist Utrillo, who had proclaimed herself the "Empress of Montmartre" is even said to have offered him the title of emperor!

11 Rue Poulbot, 18ᵉ. 01 42 64 40 10. www.daliparis.com – Open daily, 10am–6:30pm.
🆅 No. 18-04 (2 Pl. des Abbesses, 18ᵉ).

The Louxor

Don't miss this emblematic 1920s cinema with its Neo-Egyptian decor. Totally renovated, the Louxor is classed as an *art et essai* (arthouse) cinema and films from around the world are screened here, with particular emphasis on cultures of the South. There are three screens as well as a friendly café/club. Its eclectic program will appeal to both informed cinephiles and casual Parisian filmgoers.

170 Bd. Magenta, 10ᵉ. www.paris-louxor.fr
🆅 No. 09-03 (19 Rue Guerando, 9ᵉ)

67

 ALSO WORTH SEEING ON THE WAY

ÉGLISE SAINT-PIERRE DE MONTMARTRE ★★
CIMETIÈRE SAINT-VINCENT
CHÂTEAU DES BROUILLARDS

The Place du Tertre at the foot of the basilica

The Louxor

STUDIO 28

The oldest cinema in Paris that's still active has been a meeting place for many artists, painters, poets, and filmmakers. Its charm and the chandeliers designed by Cocteau have been preserved, but today Studio 28 is equipped with the latest technology. The bar in a heated winter garden, welcomes you during the cinema's opening hours.

🎬 10 Rue Tholozé, 18ᵉ. 01 46 06 36 07.
www.cinemastudio28.com
🚇 No. 18-114 (35 Rue Véron, 18ᵉ).

CAFÉ DES 2 MOULINS

Immortalized in the film *Amélie*, and a true local institution, this charming bistro offers a simple menu and a welcoming atmosphere. A not-to-be-missed detour in this typically Parisian neighbourhood.

🍴 15 Rue Lepic, 18ᵉ. 01 42 54 90 50.
Open daily, 7am–1:30pm.
🚇 No. 18-114 (35 Rue Véron, 18ᵉ).

HALLE SAINT-PIERRE

At the foot of Montmartre, this iron-and-glass building houses an art bookstore, an exhibition gallery, and a very nice bistro that's less touristy than the cafés in the area. It's very rough and ready but that's part of the place's charm.

🍴 🏛 2 Rue Ronsard, 18ᵉ. 01 42 58 72 89.
www.hallesaintpierre.org
Open daily, 10am–6pm.
🚇 No. 18-06 (Pl. Saint-Pierre, 18ᵉ).

AU RENDEZ-VOUS DES AMIS

A bar with the Montmartre village spirit awaits you at the top of the hill. Lean on the counter and sip delicious mulled wine, or enjoy onion soup, cheese, and *saucisson* – a simple, pot-luck meal, in other words.

🍸 23 Rue Gabrielle, 18ᵉ. 01 46 06 01 60.
Open daily, 8am–1:30pm.
🚇 No. 18-05 (8 Rue Tardieu, 18ᵉ).

LE FLOORS

In the perpetual competition for the best burger in Paris, Le Floors could easily come out on top. The place is quite spectacular with its 12 m (40 ft) long spiral staircase that overlooks this popular area. The burgers are 100 percent homemade (the meat is ground on the premises), the bread is crusty, and the sauces are fabulous.

🍴 100 Rue Myrha, 18ᵉ. 01 42 62 08 08.
Open Tue–Sun, 9am–2am.
🚇 No. 18-02 (25 Rue de Clignancourt, 18ᵉ).

GUERRISOL

In this temple of vintage fashion, you can find all sorts of things for almost nothing! Though, it is possible to come out empty-handed. The prices are amazing – a Saint James sweater for €5, for example.

🛍 17 Bd. de Rochechouart, 9ᵉ. 01 45 26 13 12.
Open 10am–7:30pm.
🚇 No. 09-04 (19 Rue Guerando, 9ᵉ).

68

MAMIE BLUE

The place to shop for recessionistas: little evening dressings from the 1930s–1950s, designer coats, and a very good selection of accessories. This mini-boutique, which is reminiscent of a grandmother's attic, is the perfect place to unearth real vintage pieces in good condition!

69 Rue de Rochechouart, 9ᵉ. 01 42 81 10 42.
www.mamie-vintage.com
Open Mon and Sat, 3–8pm; Tue–Fri, 11am–8pm.
No. 09-06 (81 Rue de Dunkerque, 9ᵉ).

GALERIE 9ᵉ ART

This is the place to come if you love comics. It isn't a bookstore so much as a literary relic in a road that's become a showcase for graphic-novel authors. A true Eldorado for collectors, it organizes lots of exhibitions and sales.

4 Rue Crétet, 9ᵉ. 01 42 80 50 67.
Open Tue–Sat, 2–7pm.
No. 09-17 (1 Rue Lallier , 9ᵉ).

YOOM

Everyone raves about the steamed ravioli served at this café on the Rue des Martyrs! Its prices are low, the Hong Kong-style decoration is nice, and the food is delicious. Tempted?

20 Rue des Martyrs, 9ᵉ. 01 56 92 19 10.
www.yoom.fr – Open Tue–Sat, noon–10:30pm.
No. 09-16 (24 Rue de Choron, 9ᵉ).

AUTOUR DE MIDI... ET MINUIT

A traditional restaurant on the ground floor with a jazz club in the superb little vaulted cellar. The latter revives the somewhat forgotten jazz spirit, that so marked Montmartre in its most legendary venues. Concerts are held regularly every Thursday, Friday, and Saturday.

1 Rue Ramey, 18ᵉ. 01 55 79 16 48.
www.autourdemidi.fr
Open Tue–Sun.
No. 18-02 (25 Rue de Clignancourt, 18ᵉ).

Route 4

The Countryside in Paris

A "green Paris" opens up for you between Bastille and the Château de Vincennes – a breath of fresh air! For bucolic, woodland walks and numerous gardens, take the Coulée Verte, a narrow parkway, which will take you to the gates of Paris on the edge of the Bois de Vincennes and the Parc Foral. On the Îles Daumesnil, you can smell the forest air! A little further on, the great Château de Vincennes awaits you.

....

STAGE 1 — PLACE DE LA BASTILLE

✹ A Word From Vélib'

As on route 2, you leave from Place de la Bastille, but this time you'll be heading east. Start your tour by cycling along Rue de Lyon, passing the Opéra Bastille on your left. In the distance in front of you, you'll see the clocktower of the Gare de Lyon.

Place de la Bastille

Like Place de la Nation and Place de la République, Place de la Bastille regularly hosts all kinds of demonstrations. From 1382, a fortress that served as a defence post for the capital stood here; in the 17th century, it became a state prison. On the ground, you will see lines of stones that trace its former contours. Destroyed on July 14, 1789, the Bastille is an important symbol of the fall of the French monarchy. The monument at the centre of the square, the *Colonne de Juillet* (July Column), dates from 1840. With its *Génie de la Liberté* (Spirit of Freedom), it is a reminder of the end of the tyranny, the revolutions, and freedom. On its brass shaft are engraved the names of Parisians who died fighting for the cause in 1830 and 1848.

See also p. 30 (route 2).

ⓥ No. 11-001 (2 Bd. Richard-Lenoir, 11ᵉ).

Opéra Bastille

It was François Mitterrand who, in 1982, decided on the construction of the new opera house. The building was designed by Uruguayan-born Canadian architect Carlos Ott and was built on the site of the former Gare de la Bastille. It was opened on July 14, 1789 to commemorate the bicentenary of the Revolution. The streamlined glass and grey marble building dominates the south of the square. Inside, an auditorium built from grey granite from Brittany, and oak and pear wood from China, can accommodate 2700 people. Visit the public foyers, the auditorium, and the backstage. Painters, electronics engineers, wigmakers, bookmakers – all sorts of people are hard at work in this creative space!

120 Rue de Lyon, 12ᵉ. 01 40 01 17 89. www.operadeparis.fr

ⓥ No. 12-01 (48 Bd. de la Bastille, 12ᵉ).

The Port and the Pavillon de l'Arsenal

A port in the middle of Paris – can you imagine it? Linking the Canal Saint-Martin to the Seine, the Port de l'Arsenal follows the Boulevard de Bourdon and the Boulevard de la Bastille. Cross the canal via the iron footbridge to a beautiful garden at the water's edge, with a children's play area, lawns, outdoor cafés for when the weather's fine, and pergolas covered

ON THE ITINERARY

Visit woodland Paris, leaving from the Place de
la Bastille and heading for the Promenade Plantée,
via Daumesnil and the Jardins de Reuilly, to reach
the gates of Paris and the Bois de Vincennes.

Departure point: Place de la Bastille
(No. 11-01 – 2 Bd. Richard-Lenoir, 11ᵉ)
Arrival point: Bois de Vincennes
(No. 12-124 – Route de l'Artillerie, 12ᵉ)

---

with flowering honeysuckle, roses, and clematis. A
peaceful haven where you can forget the traffic. A
short detour will take you to the Pavillon de l'Arsenal,
a former 19th-century gunpowder factory that now
houses the Centre d'Urbanisme et d'Architecture de
Paris. In this glass-roofed, 800 m² (8600 ft²) pavilion
you can visit a permanent exhibition on the urban
development of Paris, as well as temporary ones on
the future of its architecture.

21 Bd. de Morland, 4ᵉ. 01 42 76 33 97.
Open Tue–Sat. 10:30am–6:30pm; Sun 11am–7pm.
www.pavillon-arsenal.com
🆅 No. 04-05 (17 Bd. de Morland, 4ᵉ).

La Maison Rouge

Opposite the Port de l'Arsenal is a rather unusual
place: a former factory built around a residential
dwelling. Since 2004, it has housed the Fondation
Antoine-de-Galbert, devoted to contemporary art.
In its beautiful exhibition spaces, you can view
great collections, permanent and temporary;
monographic or thematic projects; and the work
of emerging talents. As a bonus, a Rose Bakery
café serves sweet and savoury snacks (Wed–Sun,
11am–6pm; brunch on weekends, early dinner Thu).

10 Bd. de la Bastille, 12ᵉ. 01 40 01 08 81.

www.lamaisonrouge.org
Open Wed–Sun, 11am–7pm (Thu 9pm).
🆅 No. 04-07 (Bd. Bourdon, 4ᵉ).

Calendar of Events

Opéra Bastille: Current program

Scan this flashcode or visit
http://blog.velib.paris.fr/en/
?s=operabastilleEN

Place de la Bastille

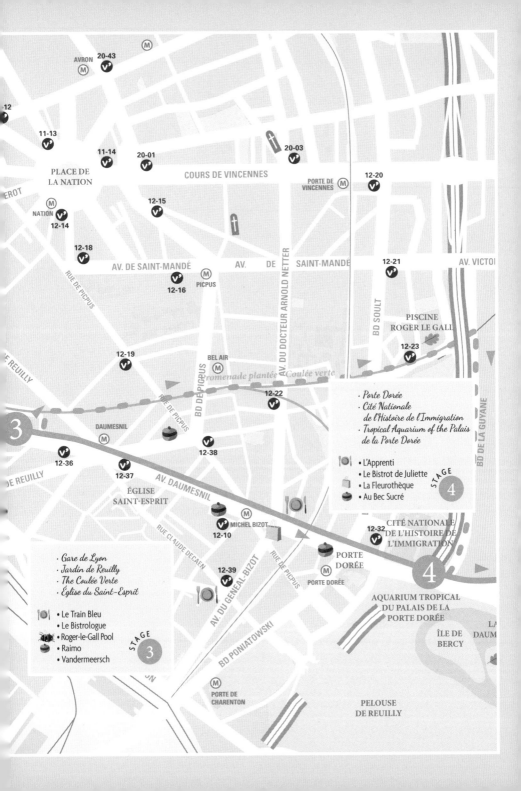

AVRON 20-43

11-13

11-14   20-01

PLACE DE
LA NATION

COURS DE VINCENNES

20-03

PORTE DE
VINCENNES   12-20

NATION
12-14

12-15

12-18

AV. DE SAINT-MANDÉ   AV.   DE   SAINT-MANDÉ   AV. VICTOR

12-21

PICPUS
12-16

BD SOULT

PISCINE
ROGER LE GALL

12-19

BEL AIR

Promenade plantée Coulée verte

12-23

RUE DE PICPUS

RUE DE PICPUS

BD DE DEPIGNUS

AV. DU DOCTEUR ARNOLD NETTER

12-22

DAUMESNIL

12-36

12-37

12-38

AV. DAUMESNIL

ÉGLISE
SAINT-ESPRIT

RUE CLAUDE DECAEN

MICHEL BIZOT
12-10

12-32

CITÉ NATIONALE
DE L'HISTOIRE DE
L'IMMIGRATION

PORTE
DORÉE

PORTE DORÉE

BD DE LA GUYANE

- Porte Dorée
- Cité Nationale
  de l'Histoire de l'Immigration
- Tropical Aquarium of the Palais
  de la Porte Dorée

🍽 • L'Apprenti
    • Le Bistrot de Juliette
📦 • La Fleurothèque
    • Au Bec Sucré

STAGE 4

- Gare de Lyon
- Jardin de Reuilly
- The Coulée Verte
- Église du Saint-Esprit

🍽 • Le Train Bleu
    • Le Bistrologue
🕷 • Roger-le-Gall Pool
    • Raimo
    • Vandermeersch

STAGE 3

12-39

AV. DU GENEAL-BIZOT

RUE DE PICPUS

AQUARIUM TROPICAL
DU PALAIS DE LA
PORTE DORÉE

ÎLE DE
BERCY

LA
DAUM

BD PONIATOWSKI

PORTE DE
CHARENTON

PELOUSE
DE REUILLY

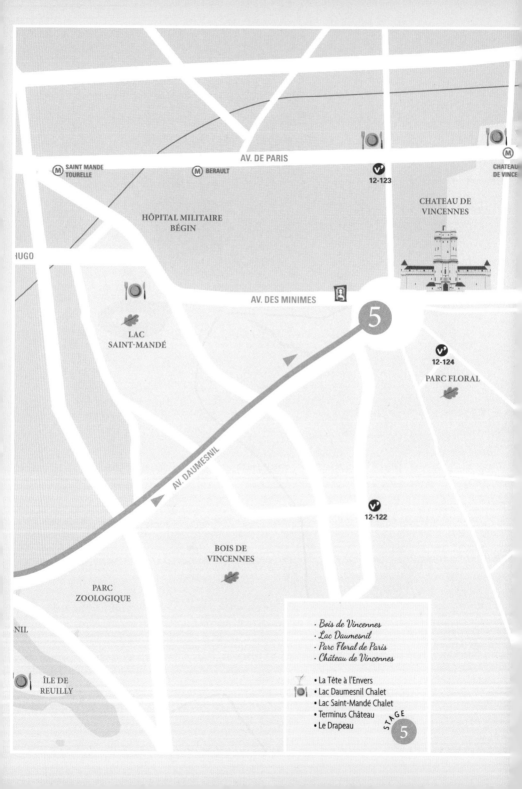

SAINT MANDE
TOURELLE

BERAULT

AV. DE PARIS

12-123

CHATEAU
DE VINCE

CHATEAU DE
VINCENNES

HÔPITAL MILITAIRE
BÉGIN

HUGO

AV. DES MINIMES

5

LAC
SAINT-MANDÉ

12-124

PARC FLORAL

AV. DAUMESNIL

12-122

BOIS DE
VINCENNES

PARC
ZOOLOGIQUE

· Bois de Vincennes
· Lac Daumesnil
· Parc Floral de Paris
· Château de Vincennes

• La Tête à l'Envers
• Lac Daumesnil Chalet
• Lac Saint-Mandé Chalet
• Terminus Château
• Le Drapeau

NIL

ÎLE DE
REUILLY

STAGE
5

Taking a Break

LA MAISON DU VÉLO

This is the best bicycle shop in Paris, and is managed in partnership with three cycling associations. Glean tips from the pros here on using a bike in the capital.

37 Bd. Bourdon, 4ᵉ. 01 49 96 52 09
Open Tue–Sat, 10am–7pm.
ⓥ No. 04-07 (Bd. Bourdon, 4ᵉ).

ROSE BAKERY CULTURE

The third Rose Bakery in Paris has set up in La Maison Rouge. The brunch menu (100% organic) features all the brand's usual fare: fabulous savoury tarts, soups of the day, smoked salmon and scrambled eggs, crumbles, scones, pancakes, etc.

🍴 10 Bd. de la Bastille, 12ᵉ. 01 46 28 21 14.
Open Wed–Sun, 11am–5pm.
ⓥ No. 12-03 (in front of 98 Quai de la Rapée, 12ᵉ).

BIMBO TOWER

If you ever wonder about the music industry's most bizarre releases, you need to come to Bimbo Tower. As a bonus, you'll also find some improbable gadgets here.

📗 5 Passage Saint-Antoine, 11ᵉ. 01 49 29 76 70.
Open Wed–Sat, 1–7pm.
ⓥ No. 11-04 (3 Rue de Charonne, 11ᵉ).

MOUMOUTE BAR

The slightty hirsute should feel at ease here, because everything in this bar is furry! The perfect place to come and warm up in a fluffy cocoon. Cuddle up with caution, or lounge with elegant nonchalance, glass in hands.

🍸 6 Pl. de la Bastille, 12ᵉ. 01 43 42 90 32.
Open daily, 9:30am–4am.
ⓥ No. 11-01 (2 Bd. Richard-Lenoir, 11ᵉ).

LE MOTEL

This indie bar in the Charonne district is a skillful mix of the latest pop-rock music, inexpensive drinks, and a quirky clientele. A small live band, DJ set, or pop quiz animates evenings that always have an intimate party feel. You'll feel right at home!

🍻 8 Passage Josset, 11ᵉ. 01 58 30 88 52.
www.lemotel.fr – Open Tue–Sun, 6pm–1:45am.
ⓥ No. 11-04 (3 Rue de Charonne, 11ᵉ).

L'ARBRE À LETTRES

Bookworms will be in heaven upon entering this great bookstore. From classics to the latest releases, art books to children's books, there's something for everyone. A picture window opening out onto a tree-shaded courtyard adds to the place's charm.

📗 62 Rue du Faubourg-Saint-Antoine, 12ᵉ.
01 53 33 83 23. www.arbrealettres.com
Open Mon–Sat, 10am–8pm; Sun 2–7pm.
ⓥ No. 11-04 (3 Rue de Charonne, 11ᵉ).

MORRY'S

Morry's is an institution for the residents of the Charonne neighbourhood. Welcome to the temple of bagels. Bacon, duck breast, cream cheese … all sorts of ingredients are good for filling these little round buns. And the bagels themselves come flavoured with olives or cumin, onions or tomatoes. Both soft and crusty, they're considered by some to be better than the authentic American variety, whose dough is sometimes pulpy and elastic.

🍽 1 Rue de Charonne, 11ᵉ. 01 48 07 03 03.
Open Mon–Sat, 9am–6pm.
ⓥ No. 11-04 (3 Rue de Charonne, 11ᵉ).

SOME GIRLS BAR

As its name suggests, the owner is a fan of the Rolling Stones. So expect a rock'n'roll vibe. The bar is located in the most festive street of the area, and its happy hour extends to 10pm. To avoid the crowds, get here early on weekend nights.

🍸 43 Rue de Lappe, 11ᵉ. 01 48 06 40 33.
Open Mon–Sat, 7pm–2am.
ⓥ No. 11-04 (3 Rue de Charonne, 11ᵉ).

La Maison du Vélo

✪ A Word From Vélib'

Don't plough to the Gare de Lyon with your head down, but rather follow the bike path slightly to your left on the Avenue Daumesnil. You'll be cycling alongside the Viaduc des Arts, which runs along the other side of the avenue. Continue on the path as far as the Jardin de Reuilly; the Promenade Plantée on the viaduct is accessible only to pedestrians on this stretch.

Faubourg Saint-Antoine

Just imagine that until the 12th century, there were swamps here! This area is often defined by its main street, the Rue du Faubourg-Saint-Antoine, which follows the ancient route linking the Bastille fortress with the Abbaye de Saint-Antoine-des-Champs (which stood on the site of the present-day Saint-Antoine hospital). In the 13th century, the abbesses who lived here were prominent figures at the heart of the neighbourhood. In its Medieval beginnings, many craftsmen set up their workshops around this road, in particular furniture specialists, such as: cabinetmakers, marquetry inlayers, bronzesmiths, and weavers… Some of the local artists and craftsmen who worked here, were: André Boulle (1642–1732), Charles Cressent (1685–1768), Jean-François Œben (1720–1763), Jean-François Leleu (1729–1807), Jean-Henri Riesener (1734–1806), and Georges Jacob (1739–1814). Today, you can still see little workshops at the bacl of courtyards, cul-de-sacs, narrow streets, and quaint alleys. Though they look like disuded, often neglected huts, but that give the area its character. In place of these old workshops, houses are going up for families of a new Bohemian bourgeoisie. And fashion ans interior design shops are popping up as well. Meander around the neighbourhood, between Rue de Charonne, Avenue Ledru-Rollin, and Rue du Faubourg-Saint-Antoine, looking for 17th-century courtyards.

The Neighbourhood's Alleys and Courtyards

After exploring the area's streets and alleys, you could also try finding its hidden passageways! A little game: see if you can find the Passage du Chantier, Passage Bel-Air, Passage de la Boule-Blanche, and Passage de la Bonne-Graine (once occupied by grain merchants). On the Passage l'Homme, grass grows among the cobblestones, and craftsmen still work on two floors. There's chairmaking, French polishing, cabinetmaking, lacquerwork, leather casings… and you can also see one of the last remaining 18th-century chimneys. Just as unusual and remarkable are the courtyards: Cours Damoye, Cours Delépine, Cours de l'Industrie, Cours de l'Ours, Cours de la Maison-Brûlée, Cours des Trois-Frères, Cours de l'Étoile-d'Or, as well as the irresistible Cours des Shadoks, named after the characters created by Jacques Rouxel, who had an office here.

Viaduc des Arts

This viaduct was designed by Patrick Berger, who used the arches of a viaduct of the old Bastille-suburb line. Today, the arcades house workshops of goldsmiths, cabinetmakers, carpetmakers, and metalworkers. You'll also find shops and studios of antique restorers, interior designers, stringed-instrument makers, jewellers, and furniture makers, etc. Note, too, the Galerie Via (Valorisation de l'innovation de l'ameublement). This association promotes contemporary interior design (furniture, lighting, tableware, carpets, textiles) and organizes a number exhibitions every year.

Viaduc des Arts

Aligre and Beauveau Markets

The Beauveau market is the covered part of the colourful and exotic Aligre market. It's worth a detour to see this part alone, which is housed in a beautiful hall with an inverted hull-shaped roof. With a less vibrant and popular atmosphere than the outside market, it has a more intimate feel. You'll find lots of regional produce here and it's the perfect place to stock up for a picnic at the end of your ride at the Bois de Vincennes! The produce is of high quality; expect to pay accordingly.

Place d'Aligre, 12ᵉ.
Tue–Sat, 9am–1pm and 3:30–7:30pm; Sun, 9am–1:30pm.
No. 12-05 (74 Rue Crozatier, 12ᵉ)

Maison des Ensembles

A key place in the history of the Aligre neighbourhood, this renovated building now houses a performance venue, an exhibition hall, and a library of photos. It also serves as the home of local associations.

3-5 Rue d'Aligre, 12ᵉ. 01 53 46 75 10. www.ligueparis.org
Open Mon–Sat, 10am–11pm (Tue midnight, Sat 2am).
No. 12-05 (74 Rue Crozatier, 12ᵉ)

ALSO WORTH SEEING ON THE WAY

ÉGLISE SAINTE-MARGUERITE ★ ★

Taking a Break

LE BARON ROUGE

One of the best wine bars in Paris, where you can eat and drink in an informal, friendly atmosphere around wine barrels that have been converted into tables. The bar also doubles as a wine shop. Food-wise, you can enjoy hams, cheeses, and even oysters here.

1 Rue Théophile-Roussel, 12ᵉ. 01 43 43 14 32.
No. 12-101 (89 Rue de Charenton, 12ᵉ).

LE CHINA

Entering here is like walking into a clandestine club of the 1930s. The retro-chic decor is perfect. A bar, restaurant, and concert and events venue, Le China inspires romance with its candles and warm lighting. On the menu are divine Asian dishes, of the sort that you won't find at your local Chinese restaurant, for €15–25.

50 Rue de Charenton, 12ᵉ. 01 43 46 08 09.
www.lechina.eu
Open Mon–Fri, noon–2am; Sat and Sun, 5pm–2am.
No. 12-101 (89 Rue de Charenton, 12ᵉ).

LA GAZZETTA

In a 1930s decor, talented Swedish chef Peter Nilsson intuitively prepares food that is simple and tasty. The presentation of the dishes is sophisticated and the recipes are revisited with Scandinavian and Mediterranean influences. The impressive wine list features wines from the south of France.

29 Rue de Cotte, 12ᵉ. 01 43 47 47 05.
lagazzetta.fr – Open Tue–Sat, noon–3pm and 7–11pm.
No. 12-101 (89 Rue de Charenton, 12ᵉ).

BLÉ SUCRÉ

Indulge your taste buds with Blé Sucré's wonderful patisseries. The cakes, as well as being delicious, are beautifully presented. So beautifully, indeed, that it's difficult to choose between all these tempting treats! Get there in the morning as by the end of the day, everyone in the area will already have enjoyed them!

7 Rue Antoine-Vollon, 12ᵉ. 01 43 40 77 73.
www.blesucre.fr
Open Tue–Sat, 7am–7:30; Sun 7am–1:30pm.
No. 12-04 (76 Rue Traversière, 12ᵉ).

LE CALBAR

Discover the art of mixology in this off-the-wall place, where beneath their dandy-like airs, the bartenders run around in their boxers! The cocktails are made with fresh ingredients, and original recipes. The results are scrumptions! Éric Robin designed the cosy yet understated interior.

82 Rue de Charenton, 12ᵉ. 01 84 06 18 90.
www.lecalbarcocktail.com
Open Mon–Fri, 3pm–1:30am; Sat, 5pm–1:30am.
No. 12-101 (89 Rue de Charenton, 12ᵉ).

Calendar of Events

More information on Paris markets
Scan this flashcode or visit
http://blog.velib.paris.fr/
en/?s=marchesparisiensEN

✪ A Word From Vélib'

Continue up Avenue Daumesnil on the same bike path. This will take you all the way to the Bois de Vincennes, but we highly recommend a detour along the part of the Promenade Plantée that's open to cyclists. Turn onto Rue Brahms, which is on your left just after the old Reuilly station. Signposts will direct you to the Promenade Plantée and Allée Vivaldi.

Gare de Lyon

This is the best known of Paris's seven stations. It was built in 1899 by the architect Marius Toudoire – who also designed other stations in France – and was enlarged in 1927. The latest renovations have been completed in 2012. Its 64 m (210 ft) tall clocktower overlooks Paris's 12th arrondissement and beyond, and its huge clock provides the time for the area's residents. Be sure to visit Le Train Bleu, the famous restaurant on the second floor of the grand hall. It was created for the World Fair of 1900, by request of the PLM (the Paris-Lyon-Marseille railway company). It was opened in 1901 by President Émile Loubet and classed as an historic monument in 1972 by André Malraux. It owes its name to the old blue Paris–Vintimille train, which used to travel from Marseille, along the French Riviera, to Nice and Monaco. Inside, the sumptuous decor of its dining rooms is laden with gilding, mouldings, chandeliers, and frescoes. Le Train bleu has numbered many famous faces among its regular clientele, included Coco Chanel, Cocteau, Dalí, Jean Gabin, Marcel Pagnol, Sarah Bernhardt, Edmond Rostand, Colette, Brigitte Bardot, and François Mitterrand.

1 Pl. Louis-Armand, 12e.
Ⓥ No. 12-06 (15 Rue Van-Gogh, 12e).

Jardin de Reuilly

Opposite the 12th arrondissement's town hall, the Jardin de Reuilly is one of the largest green spaces in southeast Paris (1.52 ha/3.76 ac), with its gently sloping paths and its thematic gardens – bamboos, heathers, ferns, Euphorbia, roses – surrounded by statues, hackberries, and green-barked maples. The garden was designed by architect Pierre Colboc and the group Paysage, who laid out the garden between 1992 and 1998 on the site of the former Reuilly freight station. In 2010, a unique public water fountain was installed at the Avenue Daumesnil entrance that distributes sparkling as well as still water: it is the first fountain of its kind in France!

15 Rue Albinoni, 12e. 01 42 76 40 40.
Ⓥ No. 12-27 (2 Rue Montgallet, 12e).

The Coulée Verte (or Promenade Plantée)

Did you know that the concept of the Coulée Verte has served as a model for similar projects elsewhere in the world, such as New York's High Line? Meandering from Bastille as far as Porte Dorée, the 4.5 km (2.8 mi) of this "planted promenade" follow the route traced by the old railway built by Napoleon III. Nine meters (30 ft) above ground, the promenade unfolds amid the surrounding rooftops, offering beautiful

Gare de Lyon

Le Train Bleu

landscapes. Arbours laden with greenery, abundant bushes, and flowerbeds bordered with lavender follow on from each other along a narrow path. Walkers, joggers, and all those who want to forget about the city below are welcome! You can bike along it on your Vélib' from point 3 (shown on the map by a dotted line).

30 Bd. Diderot, 12ᵉ. 01 43 43 53 31.

 No. 12-08 (15 Bis Rue Hector-Malot, 12ᵉ).

Église du Saint-Esprit

This church, made from reinforced concrete and with a square nave, was classed as an historic monument because of its splendid mosaics, stained-glass windows, and ironwork. Its dome was inspired by that of the Hagia Sophia in Istanbul. Architect Paul Tournon carried out the project between 1928 and 1935, at the request of Jean Verdier, Cardinal and Archbishop of Paris. It's well worth a visit.

Entrances at 186 Av. Daumesnil or 1 Rue Cannebière, 12ᵉ.

No. 12-11 (77-81 Rue Claude-Decaen, 12ᵉ).

Taking a Break

LE TRAIN BLEU

As though it were a museum, paintings by the masters adorn the gilded walls and the mouldings on the ceilings. This restaurant is set in a magnificent interior that is truly representative of France. It's hardly surprising that Coco Chanel, Brigitte Bardot, and Jean Cocteau were regulars.

Gare de Lyon, 1 Pl. Louis-Armand, 12ᵉ.
01 43 43 09 06. www.le-train-bleu.fr
Open daily, 11:30am–3pm and 7–11pm.
No. 12-151 (on the second floor on the Gare de Lyon, 12ᵉ).

LE BISTROLOGUE

This local, typically Parisian bistro serves simple but delicious food. Whether you want a quick lunch, with a salad featuring produce from the Southwest, or a more leisurely dinner, you'll find dishes brimming with flavour. Excellent value for money.

74 Bd. Diderot, 12ᵉ. 01 43 40 11 99.
Open daily, 8am–2am.
No. 12-09 (124 Rue de Charenton, 12ᵉ).

THE ROGER-LE-GALL POOL

From the Coulée Verte, you can't miss this pool, with its giant mast holding the tarp up in summertime. With the advent of good weather, the roof is retracted and the sundeck becomes available. This pool in the east of Paris is the only one in the capital allowing nude swimming. Every Monday and Wednesday night, l'Association des Naturistes de Paris – a sport club created in 1953 and affiliated with the French swimming federation – organizes naturists nights.

4 Bd. Carnot, 12ᵉ. 01 44 73 81 12.
No. 12-23 (15 Av. Émile-Laurent, 12ᵉ).

RAIMO

Its Formica bar is reminiscent of the brasseries of yesteryear, but this is above all the oldest homemade ice cream parlour in Paris, established in 1947 by an Italian family. The legendary *salon de thé* serves a selection of seasonal, original flavours (lemon and basil, coconut and mango zest …), *bombes glacées*, and *vacherins*.

63 Bd. de Reuilly, 12ᵉ. 01 43 43 70 17.
www.raimo.fr
Open Tue–Sun, 10am–10:30pm (Fri and Sat, 11:45pm).
No. 12-37 (53 Bd. de Reuilly, 12ᵉ).

VANDERMEERSCH

Baker of this bread, for which he kneads the dough, and pastry chef of all these goodies, Stéphane Vandermeersch also serves tasty breakfasts, delicious desserts, and one of his specialities, *kouglof* (gugelhupf), for when you crave just a little something sweet!

278 Av. Daumesnil, 12ᵉ. 01 43 47 21 66.
www.boulangerie-patisserie-vandermeersch.com
Open Wed–Sat, 7am–8pm; Sun, 7am–5pm.
No. 12-32 (1 Pl. Édouard-Renard, 12ᵉ).

✽ A Word From Vélib'

Pedal along Rue Brahms and take the bike path on the right. It will take you through a dark tunnel, which is the entrance to the Promenade Plantée. Then you'll find yourself in an urban forest – not an unpleasant surprise. Follow the bike path, passing under the old railway bridges, and enjoy nature as far as the gates of Paris. The route will take you alongside the perimeter road on the wide bike path of the Boulevard de la Guyane at Saint-Mandé. Keep biking straight ahead until you reach the edge of the Bois de Vincennes.

Porte Dorée

This Art Deco style palace was built for the Paris Colonial Exhibition of 1931. It is located on the Place Édouard-Renard (formerly Porte de Picpus). Admire the fountain in the middle of the square with its gilded statue of *La France*. It is the work of sculptor Léon-Ernest Drivier and was once known as *France Colonisatrice*. The reason why this gate is called *Dorée* (Golden) has nothing to do with its colour. In fact it is so named because it is situated at the entrance to the Bois de Vincennes, it's a "porte d'orée" (orée meaning edge). Lately, the square has reclaimed its palm trees, which gave visitors to the Colonial Exhibition a foretaste of exotic lands!

🅥 No. 12-32 (2 Pl. Édouard-Renard, 12ᵉ).

Cité Nationale de l'Histoire de l'Immigration

The former 1931 Colonial Exhibition pavilion, which became the Musée des Colonies, then the Musée des Arts d'Afrique et d'Océanie, today houses the first museum to be devoted to immigration and its history. Its aim is to relate and explain immigration, from the end of the 19th century onward, through all its different facets (economic, political, and linked to decolonization and wars). The permanent exhibition, or "Parcours Repères" ("Benchmarks"), presents photographs, oral testimonies, and archive documents, and also includes educational workshops.

Temporary exhibitions are also organized on different themes: identity, borders, territory, multiculturalism, etc. In the heart of the Cité, the Abdelmalek-Sayad multimedia library has 80 spaces, open and free to the public, where you can consult 20,000 reference works (books, journals, films, sound archives, and other documents) relating to the memories of immigration cultures.

Palais de la porte Dorée. 293 Av. Daumesnil, 12ᵉ.
01 53 59 58 60. www.histoire-immigration.fr
Open Tue–Sun, 10am–5:30pm (Sat and Sun 7pm).
🅥 No. 12-32 (2 Pl. Édouard-Renard, 12ᵉ).

Tropical Aquarium of the Palais de la Porte Dorée

From the creation of the former Colonial Exhibition pavilion until 1931, this place allowed visitors to discover the aquatic life of France's colonies. It now houses 5000 tropical and temperate marine species. Don't miss the crocodile pit and the colourful coral-reef fish!

Palais de la porte Dorée. 293 Av. Daumesnil, 12ᵉ.
01 53 59 58 60. www.aquarium-portedoree.fr
Open Tue–Sun, 10am–5:30pm (Sat–Sun, closes at 7pm).
🅥 No. 12-32 (2 Pl. Édouard-Renard, 12ᵉ).

ALSO WORTH SEEING ON THE WAY

PLACE DE LA NATION ★ ★

FONDATION EUGÈNE NAPOLÉON ★

MAISON D'EUROPE ET D'ORIENT (PASSAGE HENNEL) ★

PARIS
EN SCÈNE

Taking a Break

L'APPRENTI

This upmarket brasserie has helped to boost the image of great French brasseries, which have often been known for their less-than-fresh produce and prices that beggar belief. Here, the prices are still high, but the setting is cozy and the hearty meals are of an excellent standard.

🍽 257 Av. Daumesnil, 12ᵉ. 01 43 44 38 21. www.lapprenti-restaurant.com
Open daily, noon–2:30pm and 7–10pm.
Ⓥ No. 12-32 (2 Pl. Édouard-Renard, 12ᵉ).

LA FLEUROTHÈQUE

Opened more than 30 years ago, La Fleurothèque is a real local institution. The orange-fronted florist's facade has not changed its *raison d'être*. Whether you're looking for an impressive pot plant to decorate your apartment, or a bouquet to offer your sweetheart, this is the place to come for flowers with a smile!

🏬 256 Bis Av. Daumesnil, 12ᵉ. 01 43 43 32 36.
Open daily, 9am–7:30pm.
Ⓥ No. 12-32 (2 Pl. Édouard-Renard, 12ᵉ).

LE BISTROT DE JULIETTE

Near Lac Daumesnil, Le Bistrot de Juliette is a truly authentic Parisian bar/brasserie with a friendly atmosphere, hearty food, and competitive prices. You'll feel right at home.

🍽 86 Rue de Wattignies, 12ᵉ. 09 60 15 41 67 86. www.bistrotdejuliette.fr
Open daily, 7am–10pm.
Ⓥ No. 12-39 (45 Av. du Général-Michel-Bizot, 12ᵉ).

AU BEC SUCRÉ

Let yourself be tempted by the goodies on sale in this charming boulangerie. What with its *pains au chocolat aux amandes*, raspberry eclairs, and its vast selection of breads, you'll be leaving with your hands and tummy full!

🍩 254 Av. Daumesnil, 12ᵉ. 01 43 43 33 92.
Ⓥ No. 12-32 (1 Pl. Édouard-Renard, 12ᵉ).

81

⚜ A Word From Vélib'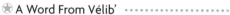

Explore the Bois de Vincennes and Lac Daumesnil, then rejoin Avenue Daumesnil to cross the wood and reach the Château de Vincennes. There you'll find Vélib' stations to leave your bike while you peruse the grounds.

Bois de Vincennes

A vestige of the forest that once surrounded Lutetia, the Gallic city that became Paris, the Bois de Vincennes later became the favourite place for royal hunts. Today, the wood is popular with Parisians, who like to come here – particulary on Sundays – to enjoy its lakes (Lac Daumesnil, Lac de Saint-Mandé, and Lac des Minimes), gardens (such as the Jardin d'Agronomie Tropicale), and its numerous paths for walking, horseriding, and cycling. Stop in front of the great pagoda, which houses the Institut International Bbouddhique. This was the former pavilion of the 1931 Colonial Exhibition; each of the 180,000 chestnut-wood roof tiles was cut with an axe! Inside, you can see a 10 m (33 ft) gilded statue of the Buddha.

🆅 No. 12-32 (2 Pl. Édouard-Renard, 12ᵉ).

Lac Daumesnil

As soon as spring arrives, Lac Daumesnil comes to life. It has two little islands that are accessible by bridge (Île de Bercy and Île de Reuilly, which has a romantic temple, waterfall and grotto). The ducks play, while people amble along.

Children can go for a poney ride, while lovers enjoy a boat trip. Next to the lake is the Pelouse de Reuilly, a large open-air area used for events of all kinds, such as the Foire du Trône (a spring fair). On the other side is the Parc Zoologique de Paris, created in 1934. The former "Zoo de Vincennes" is preparing for a new life with a new face. In fact, the zoo has been closed for renovations since 2008 and is due to reopen in 2014.

🆅 No. 12-32 (2 Pl. Édouard-Renard, 12ᵉ).

Parc Floral de Paris

Created in 1969 by landscape architect Daniel Collin, this garden of around 30 ha (74 acres) contains hundreds of flowering plant species with an infinite variety of colours and fragrances. Which do you prefer: the Jardin des Quatre Saisons, the Jardin des Dahlias, the Jardin d'Iris, or the Vallée des Fleurs? Playgrounds and attractions for children have not been forgotten, either. Also popular are the contemporary outdoor sculptures, which include Nicolas Schöffer's polished steel *Chronos*, Calder's *Stabile*, Giacometti's *Grande Femme*, Alicia Penalba's *Grand Dialogue*. A real outside exhibition! Pavilions and the huge Hall de la Pinède host exhibitions and other events several times a year. During the summer, the park is welcomes the internationally famous Paris Jazz Festival.

🆅 No. 12-32 (2 Pl. Édouard-Renard, 12ᵉ).

The woods and the lake

The rock at the Vincennes zoo

Château de Vincennes

A château that connects the ages. There are two distinctive aspects to this castle: a very noble tower, which in Medieval times was the residence of the kings of France, and a classic 17th-century castle. Recent excavations have unearthed ruins dating back to the 11th century, when the Crown took possession of the forest of Vincennes. Philippe Auguste built a mansion here, then Saint Louis added a holy chapel. The fortified part of the castle was the work of the House of Valois: Philippe VI began it and it was completed by Charles V, in 1396. On becoming governor of Vincennes in 1652, Mazarin built symmetrical pavilions for the king and queen. In 1784, the tower became a state prison. Under Napoleon, Vincennes was transformed into a powerful arsenal; it later became a military establishment under Louis-Philippe. Finally, Napoleon III commissioned Viollet-le-Duc to restore the whole castle. After all its restorations, it now appears fit for royal living!

1 Av. de Paris, Vincennes. 01 48 08 31 20. www.chateau-vincennes.fr
Open daily, 10am–5pm (6pm in summer).
No. 12-123 (Cours des Maréchaux, Vincennes).

Taking a Break

CHALET DES ÎLES DAUMESNIL

At the Chalet des Îles Daumesnil, the season and market dictate the menu. The chef's skill, the restaurant's bucolic setting (0.7 ha/1.7 acres of nature in the Bois de Vincennes), and the excellent service make this the perfect place to have a meal out or to celebrate a special occasion.
Lac Daumesnil in the Bois de Vincennes, 12ᵉ. 01 43 07 00 10. www.lechaletdesiles.com
Open daily, 9am–midnight.
No. 12-120 (Southwest side of the lake, 12ᵉ).

CHALET DU LAC SAINT-MANDÉ

This chalet, known for its architecture and history, is situated on the lake. It's a real haven of peace on the edge of the Bois de Vincennes. The restaurant serves fine food and the menu changes weekly.
Bois de Vincennes, 12ᵉ. 01 43 28 09 89. www.chaletdulac.fr – Open Thu–Mon, 2:30pm–7pm.
No. 41-602 (pl. Charles-Digeon, Saint-Mandé).

TERMINUS CHÂTEAU

Situated just opposite the Château-de-Vincennes metro station, this brasserie, which is also a hotel, serves traditional and simple French food.
The menu changes daily and the service is always friendly.
9 Av. de Nogent, Vincennes. 01 48 08 40 58.
No. 12-123 (Cours des Maréchaux, Vincennes).

LE DRAPEAU

Located close to the Château de Vincennes, this brasserie serves appetizing and varied dishes. Always fresh and seasonal, the daily specials range from tartare of salmon in the summertime to *pot-au-feu* in winter. Finish your meal on a sweet note with the fine selection of pastries.
18 Av. de Paris, Vincennes. 01 43 65 04 59.
No. 12-123 (Cours des Maréchaux, Vincennes).

LA TÊTE À L'ENVERS

This brightly coloured bar (fuchsia, dark grey, turquoise, orange...) is managed by a young and dynamic team. They'll help you discover new cocktails and beers from around the world. Also on offer are live concerts, DJ and open-mike nights, and even art openings.
Open Mon–Fri, 7am–2am; Sat and Sun, 8am–2am.
7 Av. de Nogent, Vincennes. 01 43 28 30 07.
www.latetealenvers94.com
No. 12-123 (Cours des Maréchaux, Vincennes).

83

Calendar of Events
Events at the Parc Floral and the Bois de Vincennes
Scan this flashcode or visit http://blog.velib.paris.fr/en/?s=boisdevincennesEN

Route 5

The Canals of Paris

From the Canal de l'Ourcq to Place de la République, discover an ultra-trendy "watery" Paris. Immerse yourself in areas that are on the move. Enrich your knowledge at the Cité des Sciences, greet Arletty at the Hôtel du Nord, fill up on sounds at the Cité de la Musique and the Grande Halle, have a game of *pétanque* on summer evenings on the edge of the Bassin de la Villette, then stop for a romantic moment on the new Place de la République or relax on a terrace alongside the canals, which are refreshing and bucolic in summertime.

STAGE 1 LA VILLETTE

★ A Word From Vélib'

Go the the Gates of Paris, to the Parc de la Villette. Take a Vélib' from one of the stations on Avenue Jean-Jaurès. Jump on the saddle and join the bike path of the Canal de l'Ourcq. The route is simple: ride alongside the canals until you reach the Place de la République. For the first stage, pedal along the Quai de la Marne until you reach the Bassin de la Villette.

Parc de la Villette

With an area of 55 ha (136 ac), this is the largest park in Paris. This plain is packed with activities for young and old and is bisected by the Canal de l'Ourcq.
During the summer, you can cross it on a mobile floating bridge, which is convenient and fun. Although this modern urban park lacks the charm of Paris's oldest gardens, its vast lawns are ideal for picnics or for playing a round of football. And whether it's a free concert, an open-air movie, or a parade, there's always something happening in this very trendy area.

211 Av. Jean-Jaurès, 19ᵉ. 01 40 03 75 75.
www.villette.com
🚇 No. 19-17 (99 Av. Jean-Jaurès, 19ᵉ).

Cité des Sciences et de l'Industrie

An experience that's worth a detour! At the Cité des Sciences et de l'Industrie, you're not just a spectator; you can get actively involved. Opened in 1986,

A bike ride along the Canal de l'Ourcq

The Géode and the Cité des Sciences

this museum gives you keys to understanding the world, its physical laws, the origins and history of matter, life, medecine, invention, and more. You can explore the various exhibitions and also participate in scientific conferences, debates, workshops, and games. The fun exhibitions are geared to children as well as adults. You don't need to have been a science buff in school to enjoy this place! Don't miss the planetarium, 3D film screenings, and multimedia library.

30 Av. Corentin-Cariou, 19ᵉ. 01 40 05 70 00.
www.cite-sciences.fr
Open Tue–Sun, 10am–6pm (Sun 7pm).
🅥 No. 19-09 (28 Av. Corentin-Cariou, 19ᵉ).

Cité de la Musique

Situated at the heart of the Parc de la Villette, near the Canal de l'Ourcq, the Cité de la Musique, opened in 1995, hosts international artists and promotes young European talents. More than 250 concerts are given here each year, for all types of audiences. Visit the Harmonia Mundi bookstore, the Café de la musique, the multimedia library (which has more than 100,000 documents) and the Musée de la Musique, with its rare collection of more than 4000 instruments.

221 Av. Jean-Jaurès, 19ᵉ. 01 44 84 44 84.
www.citedelamusique.fr
Open Tue–Sat, noon–6pm; Sun, 10am–6pm.
🅥 No. 19-18 (210 Av. Jean-Jaurès, 19ᵉ).

The Canal de l'Ourcq

85

DE LA VILLETTE

PARC
DE LA VILLETTE

CITÉ DE LA
MUSIQUE

PORTE
DE PANTIN

CITÉ DES
SCIENCES ET DE
L'INDUSTRIE

GRANDE
HALLE

PORTE DE
LA VILLETTE

AV. JEAN-JAURÈS

RUE PETIT

OURCQ

Canal de l'Ourcq

QUAI DE LA GIRONDE

CORENTIN CARIOU

RUE DE THIONVILLE

JAI DE LA LOIRE

AV. DES FLANDRES

RUE DE CRIMÉE

CRIMÉE

RIQUET

RUE RIQUET

RUE D'A

LE 104

901

19-104

19-19

19-18

19-17

19-123

19-11

19-15

19-14

19-08

19-07

19-06

19-05

19-01

19-02

STAGE 1

· Parc de la Villette
· Cité des Sciences
  et de l'Industrie
· Cité de la Musique
· Canal de l'Ourcq
· La Grande Halle

· My Boat
· La Plage
· Cabaret Sauvage
· La Villette Enchantée

STAGE 2

· La Villette Basin
· Le 104
· Jardin d'Eole
· Rotonde de Ledoux
· Parc des Buttes-Chaumont

· Rosa Bonheur
· Bar Ourcq
· Le Bastringue
· La Péniche Antipode
· L'Appartement
  d'Emmaus

STAGE 3

· The Saint-Martin Canal
· The Canal Locks
· Jardin Villemin

· Café Le Bonnie
· Pink Flamingo
· Mal Barré
· Les Enfants Perdus
· L'Atmosphère
· Point Éphémère
· Le Comptoir Général
· Antoine & Lili
· La Chambre aux Oiseaux

BOTZARIS Ⓜ 19-25

RUE MÉEN 19-31

PARC
DES BUTTES-CHAUMONT

RUE BOTZARIS

BUTTES CHAUMONT Ⓜ 19-24

PYRÉNÉES Ⓜ

19-101

19-21

19-114

RUE ARMAND-CARREL

RUE DE MEAUX

19-119

BOLIVAR Ⓜ

AV. SECRÉTAN

19-23

- Couvent des Récollets
- Porte Saint-Denis
- Porte Saint-Martin
- Place de la République

- Le Coq
- Chez Prune
- Adrienne et Margot
- Cuissons
- Maria Luisa
- Hôtel du Nord
- Le Tiki Lounge
- Artazart

STAGE 4

BELLEVILLE Ⓜ
10-40

10-39

RUE DE LA VILLETTE

FG DU TEMPLE

10-24

RUE SAINT-MAUR

GONCOURT Ⓜ

10-113

COLONEL FABIEN Ⓜ

10-32

AV. JEAN-JAURÈS

JAURÈS Ⓜ 19-16

RUE DE LA VILLETTE
19-16

10-38

19-102

QUAI ⒳ASSI

3

PLACE DE
STALINGRAD

STALINGRAD Ⓜ 19-03

19-102

HÔPITAL
ST-LOUIS

10-13

10-111

QUAI DE JEMMAPES

QUAI DE VALMY

10-13

LOUIS BLANC Ⓜ
10-37

RUE LOUIS-BLANC

10-31

10-36

4

10-14

19-109

10-35

BD DE LA CHAPELLE

RUE DE L'AQUEDUC

RUE LA FAYETTE

CHÂTEAU
LANDON Ⓜ

10-161

JARDIN
VILLEMIN

COUVENT DES
RÉCOLLETS

10-13

10-16

10-12

BD DE MAGE

GARE DE
L'EST Ⓜ

CHÂTEAU D'EAU Ⓜ

Canal de l'Ourcq

In the 18th century, providing Parisians with good-quality water was a real headache. At that time, a plan had already been proposed to divert water from a tributary of the Marne, the Ourcq, but engineers and developers argued so long over the project that it wasn't carried out until 1822. Until the 1960s, the Canal de l'Ourcq, like those of Saint-Denis and Saint-Martin, supplied Paris with water as well as being used for commercial navigation. Today, the canal is used only for the transport of refuse, but its banks have become a favourite leisure spot with Parisians. In summertime, a mobile bridge links the two banks of the canal between the Cité des Sciences and the Grande Halle de la Villette, to facilitate access to all the area's activities.

La Grande Halle

The former Halle aux Bœufs (meat market) was renovated by Jules de Mérindol, a student of Victor Baltard, in the 19th century at Napoleon III's request. Today the space is dedicated to major exhibitions.

211 Av. Jean-Jaurès, 19ᵉ. 01 40 03 75 75.
www.villette.com
No. 19-17 (99 Av. Jean-Jaurès, 19ᵉ).

ALSO WORTH SEEING ON THE WAY

THE ARGONAUTE ★★

ROND-POINT DES CANAUX ★

Taking a Break

CABARET SAUVAGE

Set amid the lush meadows of the Parc de la Villette, this huge marquee, which is entirely covered in red velvet, sets the tempo for nights out in northeast Paris with lots of concerts of different styles, all equally colourful. The terrace overlooking the canal adds to the relaxing nature of this musical bubble in the city.

Parc de la Villette, 211 Av. Jean-Jaurès, 19ᵉ.
01 42 09 03 09. www.cabaretsauvage.com
No. 19-46 (3 Pl. de la Porte-de-Pantin, 19ᵉ).

LA VILLETTE ENCHANTÉE

Every weekend, the latest DJs and trendy producers come here to make the steel framework of the Grande Halle de la Villette shake. This sound lab will gratify clubbers who are not already exhausted by Vélib' bike ride.

Parc de la Villette, 211 Av. Jean-Jaurès, 19ᵉ.
40 35 96 49. www.lavilletteenchantee.fr
Open Fri and Sat, 11pm–6am.
No. 19-46 (3 Pl. de la Porte-de-Pantin, 19ᵉ).

MY BOAT

On this luxurious boat, you can choose from a brasserie menu or a gastronomic one, depending on how hungry you are (and how much money you've got). Whichever option you choose, you will be embarking in a 1930s ambience with no risk of this (permanently-moored) liner sinking to the bottom of the Canal de l'Ourcq!

Parc de la Villette, 211 Av. Jean-Jaurès, 19ᵉ.
01 42 09 26 40. www.myboat.fr
No. 901 (Allée du Belvédère in Parc de la Villette).

LA PLAGE

The terrace of this bistro feels like an open-air café at night and its proximity to the canal makes you feel like you've left the city behind. Needless to say, it wont be easy to get a seat on the terrace, but the homemade tartares make it worth the effort!

41 Quai de l'Oise, 19ᵉ.
www.laplagedepaname.com
No. 19-11 (2 Rue Rouvet, 19ᵉ).

Calendar of Events

What's on in the Parc de la Villette
Scan this flashcode or visit
http://blog.velib.paris.fr/
en/?s=parc+de+la+villette

⭐ **A Word From Vélib'** ••••••••••••••••••••
Continue your bike ride along the Bassin de la Villette
on the bike path of the Quai de la Loire until you reach
the Place de Stalingrad.

La Villette Basin

A great place to meet up with friends – as
Parisians well know. With outdoor cafés,
restaurants, boat trips, and concerts, there's
plenty to do in the summertime on and around
this artificial lake (the largest in Paris, created in
1808). It's also a great place for a picnic. Those
who are game can even play *pétanque* or go
fishing. In short, there's a great atmosphere to be
had here – the countryside in Paris! Every year
in June, the Fête du Bassin de la Villette is held
here, and since 2007, Paris Plages has set up a
beach with summer-long activities. If you want to
catch a movie, there are also two MK2 cinemas:
Quai de Loire and Quai de Seine. To get from one
cinema to the other, there's a ferry crossing. It's
quite something!

🅥 No. 19-04 (4, quai de la Loire, 19ᵉ).

Le 104

This is the story of an amazing conversion.
Built in 1873 at 104 de la Rue d'Aubervilliers,
this building once housed the municipal
funeral services. Following its closure in 1998,
a restoration project was launched in 2001. The
idea? To turn the place into a multidisplinary
centre for the creation and exhibition of the
arts: theatre, cinema, video, music, culinary arts,
urban arts… Le 104 opened its doors in 2008. Its
3.9 ha (9.6 ac) of workshops, exhibitions galleries,
projection rooms, and even a hanging garden
welcome visitors. Some 30 artistic projects are
displayed each year.

5 Rue Curial, 19ᵉ. 01 53 35 50 00.
www.104.fr –Open Tue–Sun, noon–7pm.
🅥 No. 19-02 (45 Rue Riquet, 19ᵉ).

Jardin d'Éole

Are you looking for a relaxing place to go for a
picnic? This garden, with its expanses of lawns
and big tables will be sure to please. And if you
don't feel like bringing your own food, there's
a little snack bar selling sweet and savoury
pancakes, at unbeatable prices.

Entrances at Rue d'Aubervilliers and Rue du Département
(18ᵉ), and Rue Riquet (19ᵉ).
🅥 No. 18-39 (41 Rue d'Aubervilliers, 18ᵉ).

Rotonde de Ledoux

Near the "little Venice of Paris", the rotunda is,
by common consent, the most majestic of the four
tollgates of the Walls of the Farmers-General built by
Ledoux in 1784. Completed on the eve of the French
Revolution, it was never used. Opposite, on the wide
esplanade, don't miss the delightful splashing sounds
of the fountains before you settle in the sunshine to
gaze peacefully on the rippling water.
Very relaxing!

Pl. de la Bataille-de-Stalingrad, 19ᵉ.
🅥 No. 19-03 (3, quai de la Seine, 19ᵉ).

Rotonde de Ledoux

Le 104 and its artists

Parc des Buttes-Chaumont

This is without question both the steepest and most romantic park in Paris! It was Napoleon III who transformed the hill, once a bleak landscape (its name probably comes from the Latin "calvus mons" meaning "bald mountain"!) into a beautiful garden comprised of landscape scenes. Following the fashions of the time, there are little streams, a giant waterfall, suspension bridges, a fake grotto, and a large lake adorned with a rocky island and a "Sibyl" temple of Roman inspiration. It'll be some work, but you'll enjoy walking up the winding footpaths while admiring the many different species of trees and listening to the song of the birds. During the summer, the park stays open until 10pm. And a drink at Rosa Bonheur is a must!

No. 19-24 (28-30 Rue Botzaris, 19ᵉ).

Taking a Break

ROSA BONHEUR

The Rosa as the regulars call it, is a favourite amoung Parisians. You feel like you're really in the countryside here. During the summer, the place becomes a victim of its own success, especially after 8pm, but in winter, the Rosa is (a little) less popular, though still charming and with a beautiful heated and covered terrace. Get here before 7pm if you want a table, or before 10pm if you're just wanting a drink. It's worth a detour!

Parc des Buttes-Chaumont
2, Allée de la Cascade, 19ᵉ. 01 42 00 00 45.
www.rosabonheur.fr
Open Wed–Sun, noon–midnight.
No. 19-25 (80 Rue Botzaris, 19ᵉ).

L'APPARTEMENT D'EMMAÜS

The 104 arts centre houses 200 m² (2150 ft²) of vintage artifacts of all kinds belonging to the Emmaüs association. Salvage, clothing, furniture, and electical appliances at unbeatable prices: there's something for everyone! So hurry on down here – on your Vélib', of course!

104 Rue d'Aubervilliers, 19ᵉ. www.104.fr
Open Wed–Fri, 3:30–7pm; Sat, noon–7pm.
No. 19-02 (45 Rue Riquet, 19ᵉ).

Rosa Bonheur

BAR OURCQ

A terrace under the trees, the canal just 5 m (16 ft) away, a Vélib' station next door, homemade pastries, good music, low prices, and friendly staff: this place has got it all! And if you can't get a seat, you can always bring your own drinks and sit on the banks of the canal. Borrow some *boules* and make yourself at home!

68 Quai de la Loire, 19ᵉ. 01 42 40 12 26.
www.barourcq.free.fr – Open Sat, 3pm–2am; Sun, 3–10pm.
No. 19-117 (22 Rue Euryale-Dehaynin, 19ᵉ).

PÉNICHE ANTIPODE

Outfitted with a children's theatre and a concert hall, this showboat is a fun place to come! The bar fare is entirely healthy, locally made, and fair trade.

55 Quai de la Seine, 19ᵉ. 01 42 03 39 07.
www.penicheantipode.fr
No. 19-29 (51 Quai de la Seine, 19ᵉ).

LE BASTRINGUE

Le Bastringue, which recalls the *bals-musettes* (local dances) of rougher Paris, is an unpretentious bistro where you can enjoy good, well-prepared food. The owner, a true Parisian, will usher you in and make you feel like sharing a drink on the terrace.

67 Quai de la Seine, 19ᵉ. 01 42 09 89 27.
www.lebastringueparis.com
Open Mon–Fri, 9am–2am; Sat 5pm–2am; Sun, 10am–8pm.
No. 19-29 (51 Quai de la Seine, 19ᵉ).

Calendar of Events
**Paris Plages,
dates and events**
Scan this flashcode or visit
http://blog.velib.paris.fr/en/
?s=parisplagesEN

⭐ A Word From Vélib'

To get to the Canal Saint-Martin bike path, cross the Place de la Bataille-de-Stalingrad following the dedicated route markers. They'll take you to the other side of the canal: the Quai de Valmy. Then all you have to do is coast downhill!

The Saint-Martin Canal

The Canal Saint-Martin: the place for picnicking with friends on summer evenings, watching the sun set. If you're doing this cycle route during the daytime, go and have a look at the permanent exhibition alongside the canal, from the Rond-Point des Canaux to the Pont de l'Arsenal, which explains the history of the river network in Paris. It's called "*Les canaux, une histoire à découvrir, un patrimoine à respecter*" ("The canals, a history to discover, a heritage to respect"). Can you find all 12 exhibition panels?

🚲 No. 10-25 (148 Quai de Jemmapes, 10ᵉ).

The Canal Locks

The canal's locks evoke Marcel Carné's film *Hôtel du Nord* (1938), as well as Amélie's famous ricochets in the eponymous film. There are nine of them on the Saint-Martin canal, as well as two swing bridges. The locks correct the change in altitude of the *arrondissements* (administrative districts) crossed by the canal. By either blocking the water or letting it pass, they serve to control the water level and raise or lower the boats. The Canal Saint-Martin was opened in 1825 to supply Paris with drinking water and to facilitate the transportation of merchandise, provisions, and building materials. It's the only canal that is wholly located in Paris. Walkers, cyclists, and rollerskaters come here to make use of the Quai de Valmy and the Quai de Jemmapes.

Jardin Villemin

Where a military hospital from 1870 once stood, you can now enjoy a scenic stroll. The Jardin Villemin, which stretches between Avenue de Verdun Rue des Récollets, and the Canal Saint-Martin, includes a community garden that's kept by various associations. The garden contains a wide variety of trees and shrubs, including chestnuts, plane, Mexican orange, and hibiscus. In the centre, there's an artificial little lake to encourage biodiversity and attract birds. Let yourself be lulled by melodies from the bandstand, while your children enjoy the playgrounds.

🚲 No. 10-15 (46 Rue Lucien-Sampaix, 10ᵉ).

Taking a Break

POINT ÉPHÉMÈRE
Walk down to the banks of the former docks of the Canal to visit Point Éphémère, an impressive, multidisciplinary place that fosters creativity and public gatherings. You can have lunch or a drink here, see an exhibition, or attend one of the many concerts offered.
🚍 200 Quai de Valmy, 10ᵉ. 01 40 34 02 48.
www.pointephemere.org
Open daily, 6pm–midnight.
🚲 No. 10-37 (Église Saint-Joseph, 10ᵉ).

The park near the canal

The locks

LE COMPTOIR GÉNÉRAL

Under the bar's big glass roof, everyone talks to everyone else: you definitely feel like you're not in Paris here. When we came, the DJ was playing the theme of *Bagdad Café*, and we toasted with mojitos while sitting on old trunks. Afterwards, we went off to explore…

🛵 80 Quai de Jemmapes, 10ᵉ. 01 44 88 24 46.
www.lecomptoirgeneral.com
Open Fri–Sun, 11am–11pm.
Ⓥ No. 10-111 (100 Quai de Jemmapes, 10ᵉ).

PINK FLAMINGO

After hours of cycling, this place provides a moment of relaxation on the canal quayside while you wait for your pizza to arrive.
Here at the Pink Flamingo, after you've placed your order, you're given a little pink balloon so that you can be found; then you go and find somewhere to sit and wait for your pizza picnic to be delivered to you. The atmosphere is also nice inside! All the produce is fresh and the pizza dough is made from organic flour, extra virgin olive oil, and sea salt.
And best of all, Pink Flamingo makes all its deliveries by bike!

🍴 67 Rue Bichat, 10ᵉ. 01 42 02 31 70.
www.pinkflamingopizza.com
Open Tue–Sun, noon–3pm and 7–11pm.
Ⓥ No. 10-111 (100 Quai de Jemmapes, 10ᵉ).

ANTOINE & LILI

You can't miss the three green, yellow, and pink store fronts of this shop that runs along the canal. They have a great selection of fashion and decoration pieces for you and your kids.

👕 95 Quai de Valmy, 10ᵉ. 01 40 37 41 55.
www.antoineetlili.com
Open daily, 11am–8pm (Sun and Mon, 7pm).
Ⓥ No. 10-15 (46 Rue Lucien-Sampaix, 10ᵉ).

Pink Flamingo

MAL BARRÉ

"Mal Barré" is a real misnomer for this American-style café! Burgers are the speciality here: expect to pay €9-13 for a good and copious meal. The sandwiches are prepared in the kitchen, which opens onto the dining room. It's a feast for the eyes as well as the stomach!

🍴 47 Rue Lucien-Sampaix, 10ᵉ. 09 54 28 84 12.
Open daily, except Sun evening.
Ⓥ No. 10-15 (46 Rue Lucien-Sampaix, 10ᵉ).

LES ENFANTS PERDUS

A lovely neighbourhood bistro with a wonderful decor. The quality and freshness of the dishes don't come cheap, but local *bobos* flock here for the superb Sunday brunch at €25.

🍴 9 Rue des Récollets, 10ᵉ. 01 81 29 48 26.
www.les-enfants-perdus.com – Open daily, 9am–2am.
Ⓥ No. 10-16 (29 Rue des Récollets, 10ᵉ).

93

LA CHAMBRE AUX OISEAUX

The homemade jam gives a family feel to this tearoom. And the flea-market furniture lends an old-world yet modern look to this peaceful mook. You can relax in a (too?) comfortable armchair at any time of day here.
Any old excuse will do!

☕ 48 Rue Bichat, 10ᵉ. 01 40 18 98 49.
www.lachambreauxoiseaux.tumblr.com
Open Wed–Sun, 10am–6pm.
Ⓥ No. 10-111 (100 Quai de Jemmapes, 10ᵉ).

CAFÉ BONNIE

It's impossible to fall asleep here. With the kitsch decor and blind-tasting events, a fresh fruit cocktail will spruce you up to finish your tour.

🍸 9 Rue des Récollets, 10ᵉ. 01 40 35 54 51.
Open daily, 9am–2am.
Ⓥ No. 10-16 (29 Rue des Récollets, 10ᵉ).

L'ATMOSPHÈRE

The setting of this restaurant is idyllic: the well-positioned terrace faces the canal and the famous Passerelle Bichat (footbridge). As is often the case on this route, the welcome is friendly and the atmosphere relaxed. Come here for a light lunch or to enjoy a glass of wine from their selection.

🍴 49 Rue Lucien-Sampaix, 10ᵉ. 01 40 38 09 21.
www.restaurantlatmosphere.fr – Open daily, 9am–2am.
Ⓥ No. 10-15 (46 Rue Lucien-Sampaix, 10ᵉ).

⭑ A Word From Vélib' • • • • • • • • • • • • • • • • • • •

Continue your tour along the Quai de Valmy bike path. If you want to explore the new Place de la République, bear right when you reach Rue du Faubourg-du-Temple. Otherwise, continue along the canal, which becomes covered at this junction. Then keep going straight on the middle strip of the road.

Couvent des Récollets

Make a quick stop to see this building, which has been at one time or another a convent, barracks, and an austere hospice that also housed a military hospital required by Napoleon III. Located a stone's throw from the Gare de l'Est and the Gare du Nord, alongside the Canal Saint-Martin, it was much in use during the two World Wars. Today this prestigious 17th- and 18th-century building houses artists and researchers from around the world. More than 160 artists and writers from more than 80 countries have been welcomed here. Interested visitors can wander around the splendid cloister. On leaving here, glance up at the street signs on the walls: right nearby, between the Rue de Paradis and the Rue de la Fidélité, is the Passage du Désir.

148 Rue du Faubourg-Saint-Martin, 10ᵉ.
www.centre-les-recollets.com
Ⓥ No. 10-16 (29 Rue des Récollets, 10ᵉ).

Porte Saint-Denis

Located at the intersection of Rue Saint-Denis Rue du Faubourg-Saint-Denis, and the Grands Boulevards, this triumphal arch was built in 1672 on the site of a medieval gate of the walls of Charles V. Louis XIV commissioned this monument to honour his victories on the Rhine and in Franche-Comté.

Ⓥ No. 10-06 (4 Rue des Petites-Écuries, 10ᵉ).

Porte Saint-Martin

Built two years after the Porte Saint-Denis, the Porte Saint-Martin stands at the crossroads of Rue Saint-Martin Rue du Faubourg-Saint-Martin, and the Grands Boulevards (Boulevard Saint-Denis and Boulevard Saint-Martin).

Ⓥ No. 10-02 (3 Bd. de Strasbourg, 10ᵉ).

Place de la République

This is one of the largest squares in Paris. Busy both by day and night, the Place de la République is also a place for gatherings in the city. Look up and admire the bronze statue of Marianne, which, perched on its huge 15 m (49 ft) column, dominates the square. Featured on it are the symbols of Liberty, Equality, and Fraternity. The monument, which traces the history of the Republic up to its first national holiday in 1880, was built in 1883 by two brothers, Léopold and Charles Morice.

Ⓥ No. 11-37 (2 Rue Faubourg-du-Temple, 11ᵉ).

94

Place de la République

Hôtel du Nord

Taking a Break

LE TIKI LOUNGE

Time to take it easy and sip an exotic cocktail from a tiki mug as served by the bar here. Or shimmy to the island music in this bar's relaxed, "bobo-retro" ambiance. Tiki bars existed in Hawaii and on the West Coast of America before they appeared in Paris. And – the cherry on the coconut cake – a space is reserved for local groups. As you might expect, things heat up here fast.

26 Rue de la Fontaine-au-Roi, 11ᵉ. 01 55 28 57 72. www.tiki-lounge.fr – Open Tue–Sat, 6pm–2am.
No. 11-35 (140 Av. Parmentier, 11ᵉ).

ADRIANA ET MARGOT

This Polish deli, regularly frequented by a dozen or so VIPs, offers many choices. Begin with a sesame or poppy seed rolls, ask for caviar if you like, then have it filled with pastrami, smoked turkey, taramasalata, and other Polish specialities. They also serve *böreks* (triangular filo pastries). The raw herring with crème fraîche, and the Polish sauerkraut will make your mouth water as well.

14 Rue Goncourt, 11ᵉ. 01 47 00 64 50.
No. 11-35 (140 Av. Parmentier, 11ᵉ).

CUISSONS

Are you in need of a quick and tasty snack? This café serves fresh dishes and balanced meals for lovers of healthy food all day long. Popular here are the original sandwiches (€4.50), fresh salads (€4.25–7.50), and hot dishes such as *parmentier* (shepherd's pie) and *brandade de morue* (cold and potato pie).

65 Rue Saintonge, 3ᵉ. 01 44 78 96 92.
www.cuissons.fr – Open Mon–Sat, 10am–10pm.
No. 11-40 (18 Bd. du Temple, 3ᵉ).

LE COQ

Cocktails here are infused with a real Parisian spirit. The philosophy? To use original ingredients in cocktails of the moment, such as Kir royal revisited with ambrette seeds and made with Champagne from an independent producer. The bar celebrates the 1970s style of the Andy Warhol Factory. And the music's of the same era: afro-funk, jazz…

12 Rue Château-d'Eau, 10ᵉ. 01 42 40 85 68.
www.barlecoq.com – Open Mon–Sat, 6pm–2am.
No. 10-11 (3 Rue du Château-d'Eau, 10ᵉ).

MARIA LUISA

Here's a pizzeria that makes pizzas the way they're meant to be made: prepared by a Napolitan *pizzaiolo* and baked in the oven, like the delicious Bianca (well-risen dough and no tomato sauce). Those with hearty appetites can finish with a homemade dessert: tiramisu, *tartuffo, affogato*…

2 Rue Marie-et-Louise, 10ᵉ. 01 44 84 04 01.
Open daily, noon–2:30pm and 8:30–11pm.
No. 10-13 (2 Rue Alibert, 10ᵉ).

HÔTEL DU NORD

A rallying point for those that have been traipsing along the Saint-Martin Canal in their Repetto derby shoes. A cultivated yesteryear ambience, with bistro chairs, lacquered piano, and a classic menu.

102 Quai de Jemmapes, 10ᵉ. 01 40 40 78 78.
www.hoteldunord.org – Open daily, 9am–1:30pm.
No. 10-11 (3 Rue du Château-d'Eau, 10ᵉ).

ARTAZART

With its impossible-to-miss bright-orange facade, this great bookstore is unbeatable for books on photography, design, and graphics.

83 Quai de Valmy, 10ᵉ. 01 40 40 24 00.
www.artazart.com
Open daily, 10:30am–7:30pm
(Sat from 11am, Sun from 1pm).
No. 10-13 (2 Rue Alibert, 10ᵉ).

CHEZ PRUNE

A nice place to stop for a glass of wine on the terrace or, a cup of mint tea inside in the warm.

36 Rue Beaurepaire, 10ᵉ. 01 42 41 30 47.
Open daily, 10am–1:45pm.
No. 10-14 (14 Rue de Marseille, 10ᵉ).

Calendar of Events

The new Place de la République
Scan this flashcode or visit
http://blog.velib.paris.fr/en/?s=placerepubliqueEN

OBERKAMPF

⊛ A Word From Vélib' • • • • • • • • • • • • • • • •

The arrival point of this bike tour is symbolized by the flamboyant colours of the Bataclan. You can leave your Vélib' at station 11-44 to go and wander around Oberkampf or continue along the same bike path, which will take you as far as the Place de la Bastille.

Cirque d'Hiver

A circus with a solid big top that has been classed as an historic monument since 1975! Acrobats, trapeze artists, clowns, and musicians…

Join the Bouglione circus artists, who perform here each winter, for an amazing show! Originally called the Cirque Napoléon, it was built in 1852 on Rue Amelot and was inaugurated by Prince Louis-Napoléon. You can also discover the history of the Bouglione family here. At the heart of the Cirque d'hiver is a museum devoted to circus arts, where photographs, costumes, bronzes, paintings, and documents are displayed.

110 Rue Amelot, 11ᵉ. 01 47 00 28 81.
www.cirquedhiver.com
Ⓥ No. 11-43 (Pl. Pasdeloup, 11ᵉ).

Rue Oberkampf

Restaurants and live music bars flourish in this lively street, which is popular with night owls and gourmets. Situated in the heart of the old industrial districts of the east of Paris, the street could be described as a suburb in itself. From the beginning, it has been home to traders and craftsmen. In the 19th century, it was an important centre for metal, wood, and leather craftsmen. Today, the old workshops have given way to art galleries and the studios of architects, artists, and designers.

Bataclan

You can't miss it. This old *café-concert*, built in 1864, stands out with its beautiful Chinese architecture. It was classed as an historic monument in 1991. The building was originally comprised of a café, a dance hall, and a theatre, where vaudeville was performed.

Today the Bataclan hosts numerous celebrities from among the biggest names in music and comedy. The program of events includes shows, theatre, discos, and concerts. The theatre takes its name from the title of Offenbach's operetta: *Ba-Ta-Clan* !

50 Bd. Voltaire, 11ᵉ. 01 43 14 00 30. www.bataclan.fr
Ⓥ No. 11-44 (104 Bd. Richard-Lenoir, 11ᵉ).

ALSO WORTH SEEING ON THE WAY

ÉGLISE NOTRE-DAME-DE-BONNE-NOUVELLE ★ ★

Calendar of Events

What's on:
concerts in Paris
Scan this flashcode or visit
http://blog.velib.paris.fr/
en/?s=concertsparisiensEN

BARBER SHOP

Creativity and variety are this restaurant's calling card. An arty place at the very heart of Oberkampf, it is reminiscent of the trendy New York bars of Brooklyn. Its corners furnished with Chesterfield sofas and mismatched chairs give it a homelike feel. Temporary exhibitions of street or contemporary art decorate the walls, and illustrated books are available to browse. Food-wise, the dishes are appetizing and the prices affordable.

🍽 68 Av. de la République, Paris 11ᵉ. 01 47 00 12 85. www.barbershop-paris.com

🚲 No. 11-18 (87 Rue de Saint-Maur, 11ᵉ).

EAST SIDE BURGER

Catering to vegetarians and vegans, East Side Burger serves a variety of burgers, hot dogs, salads, quiches, and desserts at affordable prices. A menu rich in high-quality dishes, all made with organic produce. Now isn't that good news? Expect to pay €5.95 for a burger and between €6:30 and €11.60 for a set meal.

🍽 60 Bd. Voltaire, 11ᵉ. www.eastsideburgers.fr

Open Tue–Thu, noon–6pm; Fri and Sat, noon–8pm.

🚲 No. 11-11 (86 Bd. Richard-Lenoir, 11ᵉ).

LE KITCH

This place is the haunt of local regulars, but it reserves its best welcome for visiting Vélib' users. You need to go inside this museum of kitsch: it might be bewildering at first, but once you're in

East Side Burger

you won't be looking for the way out. Order the "Shrek": you won't be disappointed!

🍴 10 Rue Oberkampf, 11ᵉ. Open daily, 5:30pm–2am.

🚲 No. 11-43 (Pl. Pasdeloup, 11ᵉ).

AL TAGLIO

Have you ever tried truffle pizza? Don't worry – it's pretty new. But you can devour one at Al Taglio's, the friendly and destined-to-be-great *pizzaiolo* of the Parisian square. With incredibly thick and crispy crusts, high-quality ingredients freshly imported from Italy, and pizza sold by weight and in slices, this is a must!

🍽 2 Bis Rue Neuve-Popincourt, 11ᵉ. 01 43 38 12 00. www.altaglio.fr – Open Tue–Sat, noon–11pm.

🚲 No. 11-31 (1 Rue Jacquard, 11ᵉ).

AUX DEUX AMIS

At the bottom of Rue Oberkampf, enjoy a nice flass of French wine in this bar with bright orange neon lights. The local *bobos* and hipsters love it, and the tapas and other shared dishes are divine.

🍴 45 Rue Oberkampf, 11ᵉ. 01 58 30 38 13.

Open Tue–Sat, noon–11pm.

🚲 No. 11-31 (1 Rue Jacquard, 11ᵉ).

PIERRE SANG

Here you can sit at the central bar to watch the chefs preparing original tapas conceived by the bar's French–South Korean head chef, who will be recognized by viewers of the cooking program *Top Chef*.

🍴 55 Rue Oberkampf, 11ᵉ. www.pierresangboyer.com

Open Tue–Fri, noon–2pm and 7–10:30pm; Sat, 7–10:30pm.

🚲 No. 11-31 (1 Rue Jacquard, 11ᵉ).

LES MAUVAIS GARÇONS

After your long Vélib' ride, here's a place to relax and receive beauty treatments. But for once, we're not thinking of a spa for women but of men's beards! This barber is considered to be one of the best in Paris. Why not come here to get ready for a night out on Rue Oberkampf?

🗋 60 Rue Oberkampf, 11ᵉ. 01 48 05 73 58.

www.lesmauvaisgarcons.fr

Open Mon–Sat, 9:30am–7:30pm (6:30pm Mon and Sat).

🚲 No. 11-31 (1 Rue Jacquard, 11ᵉ).

Paris of the Left Bank

Go to the top of the Montparnasse Tower for a view of Paris as far as the eye can see! Then come back down to earth and cycle around the streets and alleys of Saint-Germain-des-Prés and the Latin Quarter, whose bookstores and cafés are still haunted by great writers and artists. Saunter around the places where they spent time and that many still frequent. There's a spirit of culture, history, and modernity about this lively and eminently fashionable area of Paris.

··

STAGE 1

THE MONTPARNASSE AREA

★ **A Word From Vélib'** ····················
This route starts at the foot of the Montparnasse Tower. Leave this modern neighbourhood via the Rue de Rennes to reach the heart of Saint-Germain-des-Prés.

Tour Montparnasse

What a view! With a bit of luck, if the weather's nice, you will be able to see airplanes taking off from Orly Airport, 15 km (9 mi) away. Look, too, for the Jardin Atlantique with its water jets and trees: it's built on a concrete *dalle* (large roof) that covers the rail tracks and platforms of the Gare Montparnasse – a real feat of technology. Note that the guard rail of the top floor can be pneumatically lowered in just two minutes to allow helicopters to land here. But that's not all! The 59th floor of the tower is the highest terrace in Paris, and the elevator that takes you directly up to the 56th floor is one of the fastest in Europe. It's only takes 38 seconds!

33 Av. du Maine, 15ᵉ. 01 45 38 70 54.
www.tourmontparnasse56.com
Check for opening times. Free for under-7s.
Ⓥ No. 14-01 (33 Bd. Edgar-Quinet, 14ᵉ), No. 15-118 (11 Rue de l'Arrivée, 15ᵉ), No. 15-02 (26 Av. du Maine, 15ᵉ).

Tour Montparnasse

Place de Catalogne

The plaza was designed in 1985 by the Spanish
architect Ricardo Bofill, a native of Catalonia
(Catalogne in French), hence its name. The circular
plaza follows the conventions of an architecture
already tried out in Montpellier. Its plan and the
buildings surrounding it, which were also designed
by Ricardo Bofill and Maurice Norarina, seek to
revive Classicism, with large central columns in
buildings and openings that allow the sunlight
through. The overall effect is impressive! Notice
the plaza itself, too. Completely circular, it inclines
slightly. This is no mistake: it's actually a very
contemporary sculpture created by Shamaï Haber.

🅥 n°14-114 (4 Rue Alain, 14ᵉ).

Église Notre-Dame-du-Travail

Built between 1899 and 1901 by Jules Astruc,
under the aegis of Père Soulange-Bodin, on the
site of a former church that had become too
small, this church was designed to accommodate
the different labourers that were coming to work
in Paris for the World Fair of 1900. In fact, its
monumental metal frame was reused from the
Palais de l'Industrie of the 1855 World Fair (held
at the Grand and Petit Palais). There are several
works to discover inside, including a very original
and affecting hand of the Creation.

35 Rue Guilleminot, 14ᵉ.
🅥 n°14-114 (4 Rue Alain, 14ᵉ).

Fondation Cartier

This foundation, open to the public since 1994, at
the instigation of Alain Dominique Perrin and the
sculptor César, offers a place for exchanges and
exhibitions relating to contemporary art (video,
painting, dance, graphic arts, etc.). The transparent
glass building was constructed in accordance with
the plans of its architect Jean Nouvel.

261 Bd. Raspail, 14ᵉ. 01 42 18 56 50.
www.fondation.cartier.com
Open Tue–Sun, 11am–8pm (Tue 10pm). Admission fee.
🅥 n°14-03 (2 Rue Victor-Schœlcher, 14ᵉ).

Fondation Cartier

© Jean Nouvel

VARENNE

RUE DU BAC

- The Latin Quarter
- Carrefour de l'Odéon
- Odéon – Théâtre de l'Europe
- Around the Église Saint-Séverin
- Église Saint-Sulpice
- Place and Boulevard Saint-Michel
- Musée National du Moyen Âge
- Thermes de Cluny
- Medieval Garden

- Les Pipos
- HD Diner
- Le Champollion
- Pub Saint-Germain
- Crocodisc
- Gibert Joseph
- Le Salon du Panthéon

STAGE 3

- Quartier Saint-Germain-des-Prés
- Église Saint-Germain-des-Prés
- Hôtel Lutetia
- Musée Eugène Delacroix
- École des Beaux-Arts
- Cour du Commerce Saint-André

- Chez Georges
- Les Deux Magots
- Coffee Parisien
- Ralph's
- La Crêperie des Canettes
- Coco & Co
- Le marché couvert Saint-Germain
- La Hune
- Georges & Co
- Le Plongeoir
- L'Heure Gourmande
- Le Procope
- Le Café de Flore

STAGE 2

- Tour Montparnasse
- Place de Catalogne
- Église Notre-Dame-du-Travail
- Fondation Cartier

- Le Ciel de Paris
- Tugalik
- Bagels & Brownies
- La Crêperie Josselin
- Le Nemrod
- Le Montparnasse 1900
- Le Petit Journal Montparnasse
- Le Bon Marché
- Mamie Gâteaux
- Synies's Cupcakes

STAGE 1

RUE DE VARENNE
RUE DU BAC
07-04
07-101
SÈVRE BABYLO
RUE DE BABYLONE
07-03
RUE DE SÈVRES
06-26
07-02
VANEAU
RUE DU CHERCHE-MIDI
06-04
07-01 DUROC
ST-PLACIDE
06-108
06-27
RUE DE RENNES
BD DU MONTPARNASSE
FALGUIÈRE
RUE DE VAUGIRARD
15-06
MONTPARNASSE BIENVENÜE
06-05
PASTEUR
MUSÉE BOURDELLE
15-02
15-01
15-118
BD DU MONT
14-127
MONTPARNASSE BIENVENÜE
15-03
1
EDGAR QUINET
15-04
15-115
RUE DE L'ARRIVÉE
TOUR MONTPARNASSE
14-101
BD EDGARD-Q
14-01
14-117
CIMET MONTPA
GAÎTÉ
AV. DU MAINE
14-35
14-103

BEAUX-ARTS

CITÉ

DE VI

ST-GERMAIN DES PRÉS
MUSÉE DELACROIX

ST-GERMAIN DES PRÉS

06-24

ÉGLISE ST-GERMAIN

06-15

PLACE SAINT-MICHEL

NOTRE DA

2

06-12

ST-MICHEL

06-20

06-32

RUE DU FOUR

BD ST GERMAIN

ODÉON

ST-MICHEL

MABILLON

RUE DANTO

05-33

QUAI DE MONTEBELLO

DE SÈVRES

R. DU PETIT-PONT

ST-SULPICE

06-16

05-09

06-03

3

05-01

06-22   06-28

RUE BONAPARTE

QUARTIER LATIN

CLUNY LA SORBONNE

05-08

06-103

06-31

BD ST-GERMAIN

4

ÉGLISE ST-SULPICE

THÉÂTRE DE L'ODÉON

THERMES DE CLUNY

05-02

MAUBERT MUTUALITÉ

RUE MADAME

06-17

06-29   05-30

RUE DES ÉCOLES

RUE DE VAUGIRARD

MUSÉE DU LUXEMBOURG

PALAIS DU LUXEMBOURG

SORBONNE

05-07

DE VAUGIRARD

R.GUYNEMER

05-18

06-30

RUE ST-JACQUES

06-09

JARDIN DU LUXEMBOURG

PANTHÉON

CARDINAL LEMOINE

RUE D'ASSAS

05-03   05-06

05-17

06-06

BD ST-MICHEL

05-05

06-08

RUE D'ASSAS

05

B. VAVIN

06-104   05-10

06-07

06-18

05-04

06-10

05-29

RASPAIL

02

- Jardin du Luxembourg
- Palais du Luxembourg
- Musée du Luxembourg
- Panthéon
- Rue Mouffetard
  and Place de la Contrescarpe

- Les Papilles
- Au Père Louis
- Le Café Vavin
- Chez Castel
- Bread and Roses
- Sadaharu Aoki
- Bonpoint
- Le Pavillon de La fontaine
- Le Café Fleurus
- Garden Perk

STAGE 4

BD RASPAIL

14-111

- The Montparnasse Area
- Bourdelle
- Montparnasse Cemetery

14-03

AV. DENFERT-ROCHEREAU

RUE DU

- Le Café Universel
- Falstaff
- La Closerie des Lilas
- Toritcho
- La Rotonde
- La Coupole
- Lucernaire Cinéma

STAGE 5

DENFERT
ROCHEREAU

CIEL DE PARIS
After you've climbed the hills on your Vélib', climb to the top of the Tour Montparnasse. Go to the 56th floor and catch a bird's eye view of the frenetic city below. You can even dine here and make the most of the view for an evening.

33 Av. du Maine, 15e. 01 40 64 77 64. www.cieldeparis.com – Open daily, 7:30am–11pm.
No. 15-03 (1 Bd. de Vaugirard, 15e).

LE PETIT JOURNAL MONTPARNASSE
You will appreciate the nocturnal magic of this jazz club with its friendly, cozy ambience reminiscent of an oldtime music hall. It has an eclectic musical progam and has hosted all the big names on the international scene. From country to blues, New Orleans to be-bop, all genres of jazz have featured here: auditory pleasures to appeal to all.

13 Rue du Commandant-René-Mouchotte, 14e. 01 43 21 56 70. www.petitjournalmontparnasse.com
No. 14-117 (5 Rue du Commandant-René-Mouchotte, 15e).

TUGALIK
You will savour everything in this restaurant: the cosy decor, the luxurious atmosphere, but above all the original cuisine it serves. With homemade dishes created from fresh produce, Tugalik proves that healthy eating can be an intense pleasure, whether you're vegetarian or gluten- or lactose-intolerant. The menu, which changes weekly, offers dishes created from fresh fruits, vegetables, and organic grains. Natural and delicious, convenient and inexpensive (the set lunch menu costs a mere €10 to take out or €15 to eat in), the food here is also full of exotic flavours.

29 Rue Saint-Placide, 6e. 01 42 84 02 04. www.tugalik.com – Open Mon–Sat, 10am–8pm.
No. 06-26 (28 Rue Saint-Placide, 6e).

MAMIE GÂTEAUX
If you get nostalgic for afternoons spent enjoying your grandmother's melt-in-the-mouth chocolate cakes, then this *salon de thé* was made for you! Mamie Gâteaux invites you to share the emotions of another world as you enjoy a teatime reminiscent of your childhood. The homey decor of another era is combined with recipes full of flavour, all guaranteed to bring you back to your childhood.

66 Rue du Cherche-Midi, 6e. 01 42 22 32 15. www.mamie-gateaux.com – Open Tue–Sat, 11:30am–6pm.
No. 06-26 (28 Rue Saint-Placide, 6e).

SYNIE'S CUPCAKES
Synie's serves cupcakes with a little "French touch", inventing versions flavoured with *confiture de lait* or *fleur de sel*, rose or spices, while still retaining a soft spot for the vanilla variety. This shop, with its sparklingly colourful decor, also has a dozen or so chairs so you can sit down and enjoy the cupcakes displayed in the window. Synie's pays great attention to the composition of its cakes and favours fresh, natural ingredients. These sweet cupcakes are a long way from being sickly; neither are they too creamy: the Genoise is not stodgy but melt-in-the-mouth and scented, and the icings are well executed.

Tugalik

Synie's Cupcakes

🍵 23 Rue de l'Abbé-Grégoire, 6ᵉ. 01 45 44 54 23.
www.syniescupcakes.com
Open Mon, 2–7pm; Tue–Sat, 11am–7pm.
🚲 No. 06-26 (28 Rue Saint-Placide, 6ᵉ).

BAGELS & BROWNIES
The window of Bagels & Brownies is packed with sweet temptations that will dilate your pupils, but it's the bagels that are especially popular here. Take time to choose and make up your bagel yourself behind the counter: soft, fresh white bread, multigrain, sprinkled with sesame or poppy seeds, or flavoured with cheese. Then there's the choice of filling, each more tempting than the last: roast beef, tuna, avocado, mustard sauce, chives… While you wait, American-named bagels (San Diego, Las Vegas…) are prepared on the spot.
🍽 12 Rue Notre-Dame-des-Champs, 6ᵉ.
01 42 22 44 15 – Open Mon–Sat, 9am–6pm.
🚲 No. 06-04 (19 Rue du Regard, 6ᵉ).

CRÊPERIE JOSSELIN
An authentic Breton *crêperie* in the heart of Montparnasse! The food is delicious, the decor rustic, and the service efficient. In fact, even Bretons will feel at home here! You will, however, notice one divergence from tradition: here, the galettes and crêpes are all double-size. This particularity should encourage gourmets to visit this establishment. From the most simple recipes to the most elaborate, each one is a triumph.
🍽 67 Rue du Montparnasse, 14ᵉ.
01 43 20 93 50.
Open Tue–Sun, noon–11pm.
🚲 No. 14-01 (13 Bd. Edgar-Quinet, 14ᵉ).

LE NEMROD
This is the place to come to eat an enormous plate of cold pork or a dozen oysters, accompanied by a glass of wine, before you head off for a couple of hours of shopping at Le Bon Marché.
🍽 51 Rue du Cherche-Midi, 6ᵉ. 01 45 48 17 05.
www.lenemrod.com
Open daily, 7am–midnight.
🚲 No. 06-26 (28 Rue Saint-Placide, 6ᵉ).

LE BON MARCHÉ
You'll find all the Parisian brands in this department store on the Left Bank. Have a look around Le Bon Marché's Grande Épicerie (delicatessen) to find all the latest products from around the world among products for the home and impulse items.
🛍 24 Rue de Sèvres, 7ᵉ. 01 44 39 80 00.
www.lebonmarche.com
Open Mon–Sat, 10am–8pm (Thu and Fri 9pm).
🚲 No. 07-03 (Rue Velpeau, 7ᵉ).

MONTPARNASSE 1900
Few people indeed remain unimpressed by this restaurant's main dining room. Dating to 1858, the decor hasn't changed since the Roaring Twenties. On the menu you'll discover all the usual Parisian bistro fare with plenty of affordable dishes to help you perfect your knowledge of French gastronomy.
🍽 59 Bd. du Montparnasse, 6ᵉ. 01 45 49 19 00.
www.montparnasse-1900.com
Open daily, noon–3pm and 7pm–midnight.
🚲 No. 15-01 (8 Rue de l'Arrivée, 6ᵉ)

Le Bon Marché

⊛ **A Word From Vélib'** ·····················
At the end of Rue de Rennes you will arrive at Église de Saint-Germain, the ideal place to drop your Vélib' off at the station and enjoy all that this quartier has to offer. Then take the bus lane, which is open to cyclists, on the Boulevard Saint-Germain to join the Boulevard Saint-Michel.

Quartier Saint-Germain-des-Prés

Famous names such as those of Jean-Paul Sartre, Simone de Beauvoir, Boris Vian, and Juliette Gréco still resonate in Saint-Germain-des-Prés, like the jazz that used to enliven the neighbourhood's basements! In the Middle Ages, however, this place was just a small suburb that built up around its abbey. A few centuries later, and particularly since the Second World War, the "faubourg" (suburb) of Saint-Germain had become the emblem of Parisian life of the Left Bank, a major gathering place of intellectuals and artists. No tourist should miss the two very famous cafés here: Café de Flore and Les Deux Magots. You could also hang around Brasserie Lipp in the hope of spotting Prix Goncourt jury members! Stroll around the historic streets (des Saints-Pères, Dauphine, Bonaparte, Jacob…) with their beautiful 17th-century buildings and ultra-chic antiques, decoration, and fashion boutiques.

Église Saint-Germain-des-Prés

This beautiful old church has had a checkered history. The first building on this site was probably a Roman temple. Then, in the sixth century, a basilica was built here, followed by an abbey, which soon became the richest one in France. It was destroyed several times by the Normans, restored by successive kings, then closed during the Revolution to be used for storing gunpowder. The current church is more or less all that remains of the huge 11th-century abbey. Inside, note the splendid Romanesque nave, the chancel, and the Gothic capitals. You can also listen to classical music concerts here, and the small adjoining square is a perfect resting point.

3 Pl. Saint-Germain-des-Prés, 6ᵉ. 01 55 42 81 10. www.eglise-sgp.org – Ⓥ No. 06-12 (141 Bd. Saint-Germain, 6ᵉ).

Hôtel Lutetia

This very Left Bank symbol of luxury is located opposite Le Bon Marché. And it's no coincidence! Mme Boucicaut, the owner of the shop in 1910, wanting there to be accommodation nearby to ensure that her best provincial customers would spend their gold francs here. Admire its splendid Art Deco facade, then have a drink at the bar. Fashion designer Sonia Rykiel has expertly restored the lavish interior, with its period furniture and crystal chandeliers.

45 Bd. Raspail, 6ᵉ. 01 49 54 46 46. www.lutetia.concorde-hotels.fr Ⓥ No. 71-01 (42-44 Bd. Raspail, 7ᵉ).

Musée Eugène-Delacroix

A museum entirely devoted to this master of Romanticism (1798–1863) whose portrait used to illustrate 100-franc notes. Housed in his apartment and studio (at the bottom of a lovely garden), the

Passage Dauphine

Église Saint-Germain-des-Prés

museum, which displays a number of famous paintings, has set itself the huge task of acquiring all Delacroix's engravings. You will also see some moving mementoes here, including studio furniture, toiletries, and especially, a collection of Oriental accessories and garments collected by the painter, who loved Morocco.

6 Rue de Furstenberg, 6e. 01 44 41 86 50.
www.musee-delacroix.fr – Open Wed–Mon, 9:30am–5pm.
No. 06-02 (1 Rue Saint-Benoît, 6e).

École des Beaux-Arts

The National School of Fine Arts comprises 2 ha (5 ac) of buildings (17th–20th century) situated at the heart of Saint-Germain-des-Prés, facing the Louvre. Students here are taught "artistic creation at the highest level", in workshops rather than in lecture rooms. But this is also a gallery exhibiting an incredible heritage: 2000 works by major artists (Poussin, Van Dyck, David, and Ingres…); 20,000 drawings by Dürer, Michel-Ange, Rembrandt and other 3700 sculptures, 100,000 engravings, and 70,000 photographs. All this all bequeathed by generous benefactors.

14 Rue Bonaparte, 6e. 01 47 03 50 00.
www.ensba.fr
No. 06-21 (17 Rue des Beaux-Arts, 6e).

Cour du Commerce Saint-André

This delightful arcade built in the 18th century on a *jeu de paume* court (a game like Basque pelota that was much in vogue at that time) and soon became a very popular shopping mall with politicians of the French Revolution. It has preserved some fine facades and a glass roof, which is classified as an historic monument. Enter by the fine porch at 130 Bd. Saint-Germain where you'll be greeted by two caryatids. If you go to the Cour de Rohan near the café Procope, you can see, at no. 3, the remains of the Wall of Philippe-Auguste, the oldest in Paris (2nd–7th century).

From 59 Rue Saint-André-des-Arts to 21 Rue de l'Ancienne-Comédie and 130 Bd. Saint-Germain, 6e.
No. 06-15 (10 Rue André-Mazet, 6e).

 ALSO WORTH SEEING ON THE WAY

PLACE SARTRE-BEAUVOIR ★

PLACE DE FURSTENBERG ★

Taking a Break

PROCOPE
There's a museum feel about this café which is the oldest one in Paris. Created in the 17th century by Procopio dei Coltelli, a Sicilian-born chef, it is now a world-famous restaurant. While enjoying "French cuisine with an Italian touch", you'll be able to see all sorts of slightly incongruous collectibles: caryatids, a bicorne hat and decrees that belonged to Napoleon I, fragments of wallpaper from 1830, extracts from letters by famous writers…
13 Rue de l'Ancienne-Comédie, 6e. 01 40 46 79 00.
www.procope.com
No. 06-015 (10 Rue André-Mazet, 6e).

LE PLONGEOIR
Be chic, be Parisian! This is currently the most fashionable place to drink perfumed tea, as well as to be tempted by a poached pear with speculoos cream. The *salon de thé* of the famous fashion house Hermès is housed in a former Art Deco swimming pool (Lutetia). The building,

which is classified as an historic monument, is bathed in light and offers a poetic voyage in a shop of a thousand faces. A florist has set up a studio in the window, which is a delight to look at. Silk squares and a reading room are just waiting to be touched, browsed, and admired, while foodies can relax on the *plongeoir* (diving board) with a cup of tea and a subtly flavoured pastry.
17 Rue de Sèvres, 6e. 01 42 22 80 83.
www.hermes.com – Open Mon–Sat, 10:30am–7pm.
No. 71-01 (bd Raspail, 7e).

COFFEE PARISIEN
It's difficult to give this institution a miss on a Sunday – it serves one of the best brunches in Paris! Indeed, Parisians are virtually unanimous: this is the empire of the New York-style burger. The only downside is that you need to be patient because they don't take reservations on Sundays. Come with a good book, a newspaper, and something to keep the children entertained!

📍 4 Rue Princesse, 6ᵉ. 01 43 54 18 18.
www.coffee-parisien.fr – Open daily, noon–7pm.
🚇 No. 06-12 (141 Bd. Saint-Germain, 6ᵉ).

SAINT-GERMAIN COVERED MARKET

The architecture and the beautiful arcades of this market are eye-catching. With its marble floors and magnificent shops, this market perfectly represents the Saint-Germain-des-Prés of recent times: less intellectual and more geared to shopping. You'll find no less than 30 boutiques here, mostly luxury brands. The market too is very trendy, even for fruit and vegetables. The Litchi Bar serves vegetarian drinks; you can sip cocktails made from apple, lime, and ginger, or syrups made from rose, lychee, soya milk, fresh coconut… Delicious drinks you can consume without moderation!

🛍 4 Rue Lobineau, 6ᵉ.
Open Tue–Sat, 8am–8pm; Sun, 8am–1:30pm.
🚇 No. 06-22 (17 Rue Lobineau, 6ᵉ).

RALPH'S

The new fashionable place to meet on the Left Bank, the famous American brand's distinctive building also houses a restaurant. Two wood-panelled dining rooms and a terrace hidden from view are just right for a 100% Yankee meal at any time. You'll rave over the Sunday breakfast: very good tea, tasteful pastries, unforgettable chocolate muffins, smoked salmon accompanied by eggs cooked to your liking and by two "sides". You will certainly want to try the burgers, which are directly imported from the USA, (despite their rather exhorbitant price – €27 for a classic burger).

📍 173 Bd. Saint-Germain, 6ᵉ. 01 44 77 76 00.
Open daily, noon–5pm and 7:30–11pm.
🚇 No. 06-24 (55 Rue des Saints-Pères, 6ᵉ).

LA CRÊPERIE DES CANETTES

A *crêperie* is also a friendly local restaurant. La Crêperie des Canettes is a good address in the 6th arrondissement. Here, in a typically marine interior, you can enjoy galettes and crêpes that are both tasty and generous. You will feel transported to the sea! Try these classics and homemade creations with evocative names: Raz-de-marée (Rising Tide), Winch, Écume (Surf), Mistral, Pirate, Abordage (Boarding), Mille Sabords (1000 gunports), Goélette (Galley), Babord (Portside), Flibustier (Filibuster), etc.

📍 10 Rue des Canettes, 6ᵉ. 01 43 26 27 65
www.creperiedescanettes.fr
Open Mon–Sat, noon–4pm and 7–11pm.
🚇 No. 06-12 (141 Bd. Saint-Germain, 6ᵉ).

CHEZ GEORGES

An authentic little bistro. The main room, in the basement, hosts a diverse clientele and sometimes a few concerts. It's a successful place, thanks in part to drinks at around €3! So expect to have to jostle your way in. If you're looking for an intimate wine bar, you'd do better to go elsewhere; but if you want to discover a classic, friendly bistro, you've come to the right place.

🍸 11 Rue des Canettes, 6ᵉ. 01 43 26 79 15.
Open Tue–Sat, noon–2am.
🚇 No. 06-12 (141 Bd. Saint-Germain, 6ᵉ).

COCO & CO

This is an "if you can't stand the eggs, get out of the henhouse" establishment. The place serves little else but it's hugely popular and the owner is affable too, which always helps.

11 Rue Bernard-Palissy, 6ᵉ. 01 45 44 02 52.
Open Tue–Sun lunchtime.
No. 06-32 (7 Rue du Sabot, 6ᵉ).

CAFÉ DE FLORE

This place is known worldwide and is an integral part of the legend of Saint-Germain-des-Prés. Established at the end of the 19th century, it immediately became a magnet for intellectuals of all kinds. Apollinaire made his office here, and was soon followed by Breton, Aragon, Malraux, Queneau, Vian, and all the New Wave. Although its most legendary clients remain Jean-Paul Sartre and Simone de Beauvoir, the eternal "lovers of the Flore". Frédéric Beigbeder has since founded, in 1994, the Prix de Flore, which rewards promising young authors selected by a jury of journalists.

172 Bd. Saint-Germain, 6ᵉ. 01 45 48 55 26.
www.cafedeflore.fr – Open daily, 7:30am–1:30pm.
No. 06-12 (141 Bd. Saint-Germain, 6ᵉ).

LA HUNE

To find just the book you're looking for, come to La Hune, one of the pillars of Saint-Germain-des-Prés. You'll find books on fine arts, architecture, photography, and music – all creative fields are represented here – but also all the latest novels and non-fiction titles.

16-18 Rue de l'Abbaye, 6ᵉ. 01 45 48 35 85.
Open Mon–Sat, 10am–noon; Sun, 11am–8pm.
No. 06-12 (141 Bd. Saint-Germain, 6ᵉ).

LES DEUX MAGOTS

Here lived the elite of French culture during the inter-war years. Queneau, Vian, Gréco, the Prévert brothers, Sartre and Beauvoir put the world to rights at the tables of Les Deux Magots.

6 Pl. Saint-Germain-des-Prés, 6ᵉ. 01 48 48 55 25.
www.lesdeuxmagots.fr – Open daily, 7:30am–1am.
No. 06-12 (141 Bd. Saint-Germain, 6ᵉ).

L'HEURE GOURMANDE

People always ask themselves which is the nicer here: the staff or the freshness of their homemade products? Judge for yourself, if that's possible while you're eating a brunch that should convince you totally of the quality of this tearoom.

22 Passage Dauphine, 6ᵉ. 01 46 34 00 40.
Open daily, noon–7pm.
No. 06-13 (1 Rue Jacques-Callot, 6ᵉ).

GEORGES & CO

While digital technology is gaining more and more ground in our daily lives, this shop will restore your taste for the pleasure of writing. Georges & Co's range of accessories and papers and the advice from its staff may even encourage you to pen the story of your Vélib' tour around Paris!

90 Rue du Bac, 7ᵉ. 09 81 32 33 74.
www.georgesandco.com
Open Mon, 1:30pm–7pm; Tue–Sat 10:30am–7pm.
No. 07-05 (2 Bd. Raspail, 7ᵉ).

107

⭐ A Word From Vélib'

This stage has the most winding path in the book. Ride down Boulevard Saint-Michel until you reach the Seine. After passing the Saint-Michel fountain, turn left to make a U-turn in Rue Danton. Cycle up the road, cross Boulevard Saint-Germain, and follow the cycle-route signs leading to Montparnasse. Turn left onto Rue de Condé, then take the second road on the right Rue Saint-Sulpice. In front of the church, turn left onto Rue Bonaparte, which will take you to the Gates of Le Luxembourg.

The Latin Quarter

In the 13th century, dissident masters of the University of Paris, at that time located in the cloister of Notre-Dame, moved to the Left Bank. Their classes were taught in Latin, hence the name of the quarter. The Faculty of Theology, the Sorbonne (named after its founder, Robert de Sorbon), soon won renown throughout Europe. Other universities opened here, *collèges* for poor students, then *grandes écoles* and *lycées*. This area was also at the heart of the events of May 1968. Today, there is still an incredible concentration of educational establishments around the Sorbonne. Bars, shops, and restaurants make this one of the most lively areas in Paris.

Ccarrefour de l'Odéon

"See you at the Carrefour de l'Odéon!" For decades, students, locals, and visitors heading for Saint-Germain or the Latin Quarter have met up here. You can pass by the statue of Danton, the famous Revolutionary speaker and politician (1759–1794), almost without seeing it, so hidden by view does it become with the crowds of people standing or sitting around its base.

🔵 No. 06-28 (6 Rue des Quatre-Vents, 6ᵉ).

Odéon - Théâtre de l'Europe

Peacefully situated between its little square and the Jardin du Luxembourg, this rather pompous building, one of six national theatres, has been a hotbed of political unrest! In 1779, French actors protested against Monsieur, the king's brother, who wanted to change the location of the future theatre to move it closer to the Palais du Luxembourg. During the July Revolution against King Charles X, revolutionary youth gathered here. Finally, in May 1968, it was occupied by students, who plundered the costume storehouse and roamed the demonstrations wearing Roman helmets or Renaissance costumes!

2 Rue Corneille, 6ᵉ. 01 44 85 40 40.
🔵 No. 06-17 (34 Rue de Condé, 6ᵉ).

Around the Église Saint-Séverin

The narrow streets around the Église Saint-Séverin have retained their Medieval charm, even though most of the buildings here date from the 18th and 19th centuries. They are frequented by students and tourists, who flock to the area's many restaurants. Go down Rue de la Huchette, which is the home of Caveau de la Huchette, one of Paris's first jazz clubs (1948). Stop at the church. The Hundred Years' War having left the little sixth-century Romanesque basilica in ruins, a new church was built in the Flamboyant Gothic style in the 15th and 16th centuries. Look up at the tower: you'll see Macée, built in 1412, the oldest bell in Paris! Inside are some impressive pillars and a superb collection of stained-glass windows. The large (16th-century) rose window of the West face isn't known as "hidden treasure" for nothing.

3 Rue des Prêtres-Saint-Séverin, 5ᵉ. 01 42 34 93 50.
www.saint-severin.com
🔵 n° 50-33 (42 Rue St-Séverin, 5ᵉ).

The Place and the Théâtre de l'Odéon

Église Saint-Sulpice

This is the largest church in Paris after Notre-Dame; it is even taller than the latter by 4 m (13 ft). Anne of Austria, the wife of Louis XIII, laid its first stone in 1655. But it took another 130 years for it to be completed in 1870. In between, the revolutionaries made it a secular temple of reason, and even a fodder barn for their horses. Its interior is worth a visit for its pulpit, great organ, and its amazing astonomical measuring instrument, the gnomon… But, don't be disappointed: contrary to what Dan Brown wrote in *The Da Vinci Code*, there are no mysterious symbols on the floor; nor will you find a pagan temple in the crypt!

Pl. Saint-Sulpice, 6ᵉ. 01 42 34 59 60.
www.paroisse-saint-sulpice-paris.org
Open daily, 7:30am–7:30pm.
No. 06-22 (17 Rue Lobineau, 6ᵉ), No. 06-17 (34 Rue de Condé, 6ᵉ) and No. 06-03 (15 Rue du Vieux-Colombier, 6ᵉ).

Place and Boulevard Saint-Michel

The square's large fountain, a famous meeting place, has stood at the end of Boulevard Saint-Michel (known to locals as "Boulmich") since the end of the 19th century, when the boulevard was built by Baron Haussmann. It is adorned with a sculpture depicting the Archangel Michael. You may be surprised by the number of Gibert shops you see. They are still owned and managed by the family of Joseph Gibert, a bookseller and literature teacher who first had the idea, in 1886, of opening a bookstore selling second-hand textbooks.

No. 06-20 (2 Rue Danton, 6ᵉ).

Musée National du Moyen Âge

Formerly known as the Musée de Cluny, this museum is housed in the Hôtel de Cluny, built in the 14th century to house, among others, papal legates. Mazarin lived here in 1634. It was in 1833 that Alexandre du Sommerard, Baron of the Court of Audit, settled here with his astonishing collection of Medieval art objects. He thus laid the groundwork for what would become one of the finest Medieval museums in the world. You will appreciate the artwork and the tapestries

(the famous *The Lady and the Unicorn* is here), but it's above all the furniture and everyday objects that will give you a rare glimpse into Medieval life.

6 Pl. Paul-Painlevé, 5ᵉ. 01 53 73 78 16.
www.musee-moyenage.fr
No. 05-02 (20 Rue du Sommerard, 5ᵉ).

Thermes de Cluny

The Abbot Cluny acquired the Gallo-Roman thermal baths (1st–3rd century) to build the future Hôtel de Cluny up against them. They would serve as barns and stables! In 1810, the City of Paris began restoration of the Thermes. Underground passages, baths, and gymnasiums, stretching over several hectares under Paris, were excavated and studied. This important site of Gallo-Roman civilization, the only one in Paris with its Lutetian arena is worth a visit. The frigidarium, with its original 15 m (49 ft) arch, is spectacular!

6 Pl. Paul-Painlevé, 5ᵉ. 01 53 73 78 16.
www.musee-moyenage.fr
No. 05-02 (20 Rue du Sommerard, 5ᵉ).

Medieval Garden

Although Medieval symbolism entirely guided the organization of the different areas, this is a recent garden, created by landscape designer Éric Ossart in 2000. In the Jardin des Simples Médecines, you can discover the medicinal plants used in the Middle Ages. Look at the sandstone paving: in homage to *The Lady and the Unicorn*, one of the museum's masterpieces, little footprints of the animals that have allegedly escaped from the tapestry have been left here!

6 Pl. Paul-Painlevé, 5ᵉ. 01 53 73 78 16.
www.musee-moyenage.fr
No. 05-02 (20 Rue du Sommerard, 5ᵉ).

ALSO WORTH SEEING ON THE WAY
ÉGLISE SAINT-ÉTIENNE-DU-MONT ★ ★

SALON DU PANTHÉON

This *salon de thé* is one that people like to keep a secret. You feel as though you're in your own living room, except that you have to enter the Cinéma du Panthéon and go to the second floor to get to this peaceful haven. It's the perfect place to spend a romantic moment before going to see a quality film. Entirely decorated by Catherine Deneuve and Christian Sapet, this 150 m² (1615 ft²) loft also has a heated terrace.

🍵 13 Rue Victor-Cousin, 5ᵉ. 01 40 46 01 21.

ⓥ No. 51-06 (22 Rue Cujas, 5ᵉ).

LE CHAMPOLLION

Le Champollion, or "Champo" for short, is unique in its genre: established in 1938 on the site of a former bookstore, it is one of the rare cinemas to screen only "old movies". You can also discover the great classics of French cinema and world films. François Truffaut declared that this cinema was his "headquarters" while Claude Chabrol claimed it was his "second univeristy". And you?

🏛 51 Rue des Écoles, 5ᵉ. 01 43 54 51 60.

www.lechampo.com

ⓥ No. 05-30 (5 Rue de la Sorbonne, 5ᵉ).

LES PIPOS

You'll find this good wine bar at the heart of the 5th arrondissement, near Paris's tourist hotspots. The bar serves regional produce, from the wine list (house selection) to the brasserie menu, giving you the chance to taste regional specialities. Although the focus of the dishes is on the Auvergne, the place feels like a true Parisian bistro.

🍷 2 Rue de l'École-Polytechnique, 5ᵉ. 01 43 54 11 40.

www.les-pipos.com

Open Mon–Fri, 9:30am–2am; Sat, noon–2am.

ⓥ No. 05-17 (17 Rue Descartes, 5ᵉ).

HD DINER

Immerse yourself in the heart of 1950s America in this diner that fills up every day. You'll find a wonderfully clichéed ambience, very good milkshakes, and American produce on the menu.

🍽 25 Rue Francisque-Gay, 6ᵉ. 01 43 29 67 07.

www.happydaysdiner.com – Open daily, 9am–midnight.

ⓥ No. 06-20 (2 Rue Danton, 6ᵉ).

CROCODISC

Crocodisc sells vinyls of every style, except classical. They have three outlets in the Latin Quarter offering rock, world music, jazz, Black music and more. You can't miss the shopfront, which is decorated with a fine crocodile. If you're afraid of getting lost among the thousands of records here, ask one of the sales assistants for advice. Unlike the alligators, they won't bite.

🎵 42 Rue des Écoles, 5ᵉ. 01 43 54 47 95.

www.crocodisc.com – Open Tue–Sat, 11am–7pm.

ⓥ No. 05-07 (39 Rue des Écoles, 5ᵉ).

GIBERT JOSEPH

You'll find lots of bookstore in the quarter offering all sorts of books from all over the world. This five-storey one sells both new and second-hand books. Don't hesitate to ask the booksellers for a good title: they know the place and its stock like the back of their hands.

📕 26 Bd. Saint-Michel, 6ᵉ. 01 44 41 88 88.

www.gibertjoseph.com – Open Mon–Sat, 10am–8pm.

ⓥ No. 06-31 (5 Rue Pierre-Sarrazin, 6ᵉ).

LE PUB SAINT-GERMAIN

Le Pub Saint-Germain has managed to adapt its style to that of the quarter, distancing itself from the usual image of a "pub". The merit of this establishment is that it serves very good cocktails and offers you the chance to spend the evening in an atmosphere of subdued lighting with music selected by the DJ.

🍸 17 Rue de l'Ancienne-Comédie, 6ᵉ. 01 56 81 13 13.

www.lepubparis.com – Open daily, 8am–6am.

ⓥ No. 06-15 (10 Rue André-Mazet, 6ᵉ).

4 LE LUXEMBOURG

🚲 A Word From Vélib' ••••••••••••••••••

After having taken advantage of the Left Bank's most beautiful garden, get back on your Vélib' and take the bike path on Rue Guynemer. Continue for a few metres along Rue d'Assas and then turn right onto Rue Vavin. Finally, take the bus lane on Boulevard Raspail and continue straight ahead until you reach Montparnasse cemetery.

Jardin du Luxembourg

A haven of peace in the middle of the busy Latin Quarter, this magnificent park with both French-style and English-style elements, was created in the 17th century. Go shopping for gourmet snacks at one of the sublime patisseries nearby (Hermé, Mulot, Hévin, Dalloyau…), then find some chairs or a bench in a charming corner of this garden where you can enjoy them. You'll find such a place easily, under the shade of the trees, and surrounded by statues of the queens of France. There's also a large pond surrounded by palm trees, oleanders, and orange trees. Note that the park provides excellent gardening and beekeeping courses. And don't miss the most romantic spot in the garden: the Medicis fountain!

Entrances: 2 Rue Auguste-Comte, 6ᵉ;
Pl. Edmond-Rostand, 6ᵉ; rue Guynemer, 6ᵉ.
www.paris.fr and www.senat.fr/visite/jardin
🚲 No. 06-17 (34 Rue de Condé, 6ᵉ), 🚲 No. 06-09 (26 Rue Guynemer, 6ᵉ) and 🚲 No. 05-03 (9 Rue Le-Goff, 6ᵉ).

Palais du Luxembourg

The regent Marie de Medicis had this palace built in 1612 to live here with her son, King Louis XIII, who was then still a child. It remained in the royal family until the French Revolution, which turned it into a prison. It was later reestablished as a palace and under Napoleon III became the seat of the Senate, one of the two parliamentary assemblies. Nearby, the Petit Palais, a splendid mansion, is home to the President of the Senate. When you leave, go and have a look at the railings surrounding the garden; they serve as a support for often remarkable photographic exhibitions.

15 Rue de Vaugirard, 6ᵉ.
01 42 34 20 00. www.senat.fr
🚲 No. 06-17 (34 Rue de Condé, 6ᵉ).

Musée du Luxembourg

Housed in a wing of the Palais du Luxembourg, this museum has existed since the 18th century. At that time, it was devoted to modern art, but it lost this vocation in the 1930s to the Palais de Tokyo. It now holds temporary exhibitions focused on Renaissance art that are very popular – avoid the long Sunday lines!

19 Rue de Vaugirard, 6ᵉ.
01 40 13 62 00.
www.museeduluxembourg.fr
🚲 No. 06-17 (34 Rue de Condé, 6ᵉ).

The Jardin du Luxembourg

Rue Mouffetard

Panthéon

This imposing and famous monument is the perfect example of the complicated relationship that France has had with the Church throughout its history. Designed in the 18th century as a church, the building became a secular monument during the Revolution. It houses the tombs of esteemed scholars, artists, philosophers, and writers, including Rousseau, Voltaire, Zola, Dumas, Hugo, Malraux, Jean Moulin, and Pierre and Marie Curie.

Place du Panthéon, 5ᵉ.
www.pantheon.monuments-nationaux.fr
Open daily, 10am–6pm.
No. 05-12 (20 Rue de l'Estrapade, 5ᵉ).

Rue Mouffetard

You could think you were in a Medieval village, everything is so tightly packed together! This ancient (1st-century) street descends the hill of Sainte-Geneviève, from Place de la Contrescarpe to Église Saint-Médard. At the top is the nightlife area; at the bottom, gourmet food shops and fashion boutiques. At n° 60, admire the Pot-de-Fer (17th-century) fountain.

No. 05-16 (1 Rue de Thouin, 5ᵉ).

ALSO WORTH SEEING ON THE WAY
THE OBSERVATORY

Taking a Break

BREAD AND ROSES

In this bakery/café/delicatessen, bread is given special attention. It is made according to traditional methods, using organic flours and old machinery. The result? A whole medley of original and delicious breads, including *ficelle* (a sort of thin French stick) with raisins and muesli bread. You will particularly like their organic bread, their devilishly creamy cakes, and their little tarts (which are enough to make a nutritionist turn pale!) Go on, succumb to the temptation of a Mont Blanc, with *crème de marrons* covering a crunchy centre, to take away and enjoy on the sunny lawns of the Jardin du Luxembourg!

62 Rue Madame, 6ᵉ. 01 42 22 06 06.
www.breadandroses.fr
Open Mon–Sat, 8am–7:15pm.
No. 06-09 (26 Rue Guynemer, 6ᵉ).

SADAHARU AOKI

To cross the threshold of Aoki is to enter into a sublime world. Both visually and taste-wise, everything is perfectly balanced. At the helm is a great Japanese chef who combines French *savoir-faire* with the produce of his country. There is nothing like the flavours of his *macarons* – the house speciality – to transport your tastebuds: Matcha green tea, violet, blackcurrant, salted caramel, lemon… The shell is incredibly crispy while the filling melts in your mouth. You'll also discover little biscuits, such as chocolate diamonds, dark chocolate orange slices, and *chocorons* (a chocolate and *macaron* mix), as well as a fine selection of teas. This place is a must for an exotic little break!

35 Rue de Vaugirard, 6ᵉ. 01 45 44 48 90.
www.sadaharuaoki.com
Open Tue–Sat, 11am–7pm; Sun, 10am–6pm.
No. 06-30 (22 Rue d'Assas, 6ᵉ)
and No. 06-17 (34 Rue de Condé, 6ᵉ).

LE FLEURUS

A stone's throw from the Jardin du Luxembourg, this café has a typical Saint-Germain-des-Prés feel. It's a very pleasant place to enjoy a coffee or a beer and there's even a sunny terrace.

2 Rue de Fleurus, 6ᵉ. 01 45 44 79 79.
No. 06-09 (26 Rue Guynemer, 6ᵉ).

The Panthéon

LES PAPILLES

The walls of this bistro are covered with bottles of wine. Needless to say, the selection is excellent! But people don't come here only to enjoy fine wines: the menus change every week and give you the chance to make some real culinary discoveries!

🍸 30 Rue Gay-Lussac, 5ᵉ. 01 43 25 20 79.
www.lespapillesparis.fr
Open Tue–Sat, noon–2pm and 7–10pm.
Ⓥ No. 05-05 (27 Rue Gay-Lussac, 5ᵉ).

GARDEN PERK

Fans of the *Friends* TV show will quickly get the spirit of this place: a little café where you can eat bagels and muffins with your friends, and order an American soda or a caffè latte without budging from your sofa – it's straight out of the New York series.

🍵 21 Rue Cujas, 5ᵉ.
Open Mon–Fri, 9am–7:30pm; Sat, 11am–7:30pm.
Ⓥ No. 05-106 (22 Rue Cujas, 5ᵉ).

BONPOINT

This is the best-kept secret of mothers of the Left Bank. At the back of the Bonpoint boutique on Rue de Tournon, you'll find Emma's tearoom in the magnificent setting of a former private mansion. In the small paved courtyard, under the chestnut tree, children and their parents alike enjoy madeleines, candies, scones, cupcakes, and other sweet treats. And on leaving you can stick your hand in the big glass jars and draw out a Tagada strawberry or a tangy lollipop.

🍵 6 Rue de Tournon, 6ᵉ. 01 40 51 98 20.
www.bonpoint.com – Open Mon–Sat, 9am–7pm.

CHEZ CASTEL

An institution of Parisian nightlife, frequented by everyone who is anyone in Paris. You have to earn a place here as it's a very exclusive private club, but in Paris nothing is impossible! Who knows? Maybe you, too, will get to spend a night here, like Françoise Sagan and Mick Jagger in their day!

🍸 15 Rue Princesse, 6ᵉ. 01 40 51 52 80.
www.castelparis.com – Open Tue–Sat, 11pm–6am.
Ⓥ No. 06-22 (17 Rue Lobineau, 6ᵉ).

CAFÉ VAVIN

Whether it's a hot chocolate, a glass of wine, or dinner you're after, this brasserie will satisfy your desires. If you want to sit on the terrace, you'll have to squeeze in among the students of the area who come here for a break.

🍽 18 Rue Vavin, 6ᵉ. 01 43 26 67 47.
Open Mon–Sat, 7am–midnight; Sun, 9am–midnight.
Ⓥ No. 06-07 (18 Rue Bréa, 6ᵉ).

PAVILLON DE LA FONTAINE

If you're spending your afternoon in the Jardin du Luxembourg and have no desire to leave it to go find food and drink, this snack bar will be just what you need. Find yourself a seat on the terrace and, if you're lucky, enjoy some music from the bandstand neaby.

🍵 In the Jardin du Luxembourg. Open daily, 8am–9pm.
Ⓥ No. 05-03 (9 Rue Le-Goff, 5ᵉ).

AU PÈRE LOUIS

Do you dream of tasting Bourgogne snails accompanied by a good glass of wine? If so, you can't do better than here! The establishment isn't touristy, but you'll find all the classics of French gastronomy, including *magret de canard*, *cassoulet*, charcuteries and good cheeses.

🍸 38 Rue Monsieur-le-Prince, 6ᵉ. 01 43 26 54 14.
www.auperelouis.com
Open daily, noon–3pm and 6pm–1am.
Ⓥ No. 06-29 (1 Rue de Vaugirard, 6ᵉ).

113

Calendar of Events

Fin out more about Parisian palaces
Scan this flashcode or visit
http://blog.velib.paris.fr/en/
?s=palacesparisEN

⭐ A Word From Vélib' ••••••••••••••••••

You've arrived in the Raspail quarter, the arrival point of this bike route. If you wish, you can continue your ride along on this bike path: it will take you to the Porte de Vanves.

The Montparnasse Area

This was the artists' quarter during the Belle Époque. Many artists – painters, sculptors, and writers – migrated from Montmartre to Montparnasse and took up residence in the area's cafés and restaurants. Picasso, Foujita, Aragon, Cocteau, Sartre, and Simone de Beauvoir could all be seen here. The legendary La Coupole brasserie was decorated by 27 in-vogue artists, and dances held there were all the rage. Le Dôme was the literary café of the English and Americans. Philosophy evenings were held at Le Sélect. The Surrealists met up at La Rotonde. Paul Fort played chess with Lenin at the Closerie des Lilas. Today, intellectuals and publishers of the Left Bank still enjoy these places.

Bourdelle

Everything on Bourdelle and nothing but! Visit the workshop that has become a museum of the famous sculptor who worked with the great masters, including Rodin, with whom he created a sculpture course at Montparnasse. There's an incredible wealth of material here: 15,000 photographs, 3000 sculptures, 4000 drawings, paintings, and pastels, not to mention plaster casts of the master's monumental works, which are exhibited in the Grand Hall, an impressive concrete nave!

Musée Bourdelle

18 Rue Antoine-Bourdelle, 15ᵉ. 01 49 54 73 73.
www.bourdelle.paris.fr – Open Tue–Sun, 10am–6pm.
Free entrance to permanent collections.
Ⓥ No. 15-02 (26 Av. du Maine, 15ᵉ).

Montparnasse Cemetery

In the past, the cemetery was situated outside the city. Like the other large Parisian cemeteries, it was created in 1824 to replace the old cemetery of Les Innocents, which was closed by royal decree. Covering an area of nearly 19 ha (47 ac), it is one of the largest green spaces in Paris. Those interested in finding the tombs of famous people can get a list at the entrance. Stroll around the shaded pathways to pay a posthumous visit to Jim Morrison or Serge Gainsbourg…
Ⓥ No. 15-02 (4 Bd. Edgar Quinet, 14ᵉ).

114

 Taking a Break

LUCERNAIRE CINÉMA
The Lucernaire cultural centre, housed in a disused factory, is a hub of activity centred around the arts. It aims to foster exchanges between cinema, theatre, photography and gastronomy. The watchword here is quality. Categorized as an "Art et Essai" (arthouse) cinema with the distinction "Recherche et Découverte" (research and discovery), Lucernaire gives priority to screening French and foreign auteur films, with a special focus on cinema "du Sud" (of the south of France).
53 Rue Notre-Dame-des-Champs, 6ᵉ. 01 42 22 26 50. www.lelurcenaire.fr
No. 06-07 (18 Rue Bréa, 6ᵉ).

CAFÉ UNIVERSEL
One of the best places to hear vocal jazz in Paris, this centre of live music is a hangout for young artists, who come here to unwind in its relaxed atmosphere. Situated away from the hustle and bustle of the Latin Quarter, this warm, friendly pub is well known to jazz lovers, but also to fans of swing, blues, bossa and soul. Don't be fooled by the place's neon lights and kitsch decor: its eclectic, young, and enthusiastic clientele come here with no preconceived ideas to warm themselves up to the rhythm of the improvisations and songs on offer.
Open Mon–Fri, 8:30am–1am; Sat, 4:30pm–1am; Sun, 1:30pm–1am. 267 Rue Saint-Jacques, 5ᵉ. 01 43 25 74 20. www.cafeuniversel.com
No. 05-04 (272 Rue Saint-Jacques, 5ᵉ).

LA CLOSERIE DES LILAS
Discover the wood panelling and the tables named after writers in the brasserie here. Or dine out in style under the arbour in the restaurant. This quintessential Parisian brasserie also becomes a piano-bar on some evenings.
171 Bd. du Montparnasse, 6ᵉ. 01 40 51 34 50. www.closeriedeslilas.fr
Open daily, noon–2pm and 7–9pm.
No. 05-29 (41 Av. Georges-Bernanos, 5ᵉ).

TORITCHO
A Japanese institution for decades, this restaurant will introduce you to the real art of sushi. The menu clearly distinguishes itself from that of run-of-the-mill Japanese restaurants. Count on paying around €30 per person to sample true Japanese culinary tradition.
41 Rue du Montparnasse, 14ᵉ. 01 43 21 29 97. Open Mon–Sat, 9am–6pm.
No. 06-07 (18 Rue Bréa, 6ᵉ).

LA ROTONDE
You can enjoy traditional dishes or excellent seafood platters here at any time of day. The set menus are reasonably priced considering the area, and will be served to you by very professional waiters.
105 Bd. du Montparnasse, 6ᵉ. 01 43 26 48 26. www.rotondemontparnasse.com – Open, 8am–midnight.
No. 06-07 (18 Rue Bréa, 6ᵉ).

LA COUPOLE
The huge dining room has kept its magnificent Art Deco ambience with banquettes, painted pillars, and chandeliers. Enjoy good French cuisine or brunch in style on Sundays.
102 Bd. du Montparnasse, 6ᵉ. 01 43 20 14 20. www.lacoupole-paris.com
Open daily, 8:30am–midnight.
No. 06-07 (18 Rue Bréa, 6ᵉ).

FALSTAFF
Beer is like good wine: it should be savoured! Here you can taste new types of beer and succumb to a burger if you wish. We promise we'll close our eyes to how many calories you've consumed!
42 Rue du Montparnasse, 14ᵉ. 01 43 35 38 29. Open daily, 8:30am–5am.
No. 06-05 (40 Rue du Montparnasse, 6ᵉ).

Route 7

From Contemporary to Authentic Paris

From Bercy, cross the Seine and discover Paris of the future; a melting-pot of many cultures. This area has seen one of the largest development projects in the capital, with ultramodern architecture. Wander around the delightful Butte-aux-Cailles before heading for the neighbourhood of Denfert-Rochereau, which will welcome you at the end of your bike tour.

....

1 BERCY

⊛ A Word From Vélib' ••••••••••••••••••••

Head to the huge Palais Omnisport de Paris-Bercy and the imposing Ministry of Finance building. From here, follow the bike path to arrive quickly on the Bercy bridge, and cross the Seine under the steel arches of the elevated metro line.

The Village and the Palais Omnisports de Paris-Bercy

In the 1970s and '80s, the City of Paris wanted to create a new district in the east of Paris: Paris-Bercy. This era of change was initiated with the building of the Palais Omnisports de Paris-Bercy (POPB) in 1984, followed by the Ministry of Finance in 1989. The POPB hosts all sorts of events, both cultural and sports-related, including large-scale aquatic displays made possible by its groundbreaking technical amenities. Equipped with many additional spaces, including an ice-skating rink, it can accommodate up to 18,000 spectators. Until the beginning of the 20th century, the village of Bercy was one of the most important warehouse and trade centres for the wine industry in the world. Crowds of working-class and high-society people flocked to the *guinguettes* on the banks of the Seine in "joyeux Bercy", where wine was much cheaper than in Paris! With the development of transportation, business dwindled

and the place was left more or less abandoned. It's now received a second life, though.

8 Bd. de Bercy, 12ᵉ. 01 40 02 60 60. www.bercy.fr
Ⓥ No. 12-25 (opposite 14 Pl. du Bataillon-du-Pacifique, 12ᵉ).

Parc de Bercy

The park was built on the site of former wine warehouses. Whether you want to walk, play games, or relax, you'll enjoy these 12 ha (30 ac) of contemporary gardens linked by footpaths. Skateboarders and rollerbladers can launch off from the beaten-earth esplanade at the foot of the POPB steps; nature-lovers will take delight in the flowerbeds, the orangery, the rose gardens, and vegetable garden; lovers, meanwhile, can take

Bercy and its sloping lawns

ON THE ITINERARY

Visit the changing cultures tof Paris around Bercy, the modern-day Seine, Place d'Italie, Butte-aux-Cailles, and Denfert-Rochereau.

Departure Point: Bercy
(No. 2-25 – 14 Pl. du Bataillon-du-Pacifique, 12e)
Arrival point: Place Denfert-Rochereau
(No. 14-05 – 2 Av. René-Coty, 14e)

refuge in the Jardin Romantique or converse in the Jardin du Philosophe. Don't miss the fountains of the original *Canyoneaustrate*, a sculpture–fountain created in 1988 by Gérard Singer. Next to the Quai de Bercy, go and see the 18th-century remains of the Petit Château de Bercy, which escaped the demolition of the wine warehouses around 1990.

128 Quai de Bercy, 12e.
Ⓥ No. 12-31 (49 Rue Gabriel-Lame, 12e).

Cinémathèque Française

Just before the Second World War, a couple of cinephiles, Henri Langlois and Georges Franju, began to collect old films and film memorabilia (posters, costumes, set props, etc.). Their passion led to the birth of the Cinémathèque française and the Musée du Cinéma. In 2005, following a number of moves and incidents, including a fire at the Trocadéro, the Cinémathèque settled on Rue de Bercy, in the very contemporary building that had been designed in 1993 by architect Franck O. Gehry for the American Center (which closed its doors in 1996). Visit the rooms with "deconstructed" levels, where anthology films are screened and fabulous objects from the collections displayed.

51 Rue de Bercy, 13e. 01 71 19 33 33.
www.cinematheque.fr
Open Mon–Sat, noon–7pm; Sun, 10am–8pm.
Ⓥ No. 12-26 (61 Rue de Bercy, 12e).

Cour Saint-Émilion

This unusual shopping centre has the feel of a really clean village. Its shops and restaurants are set up in the original 42 white-stone wine warehouses, which were renovated in the 1990s. More than ten million visitors stroll along the paved main street and the adjacent pedestrian walkways of Bercy Village every year! When you've had enough of restaurants and shopping, why not go and take in a film at the UGC-Cité-Ciné-Bercy? It's one of the largest cinema complexes in Europe, housed

Cour Saint-Émilion

VAVIN Ⓜ

BD DU MONTPARNASSE

RASPAIL Ⓜ

14-02 🅥

PORT ROYAL ⓇⒺⓇ 🅥
05-29

HÔPITAL DU VAL-DE-GRÂCE

BD DE PORT-ROYAL

CARRIERE DES CAPUCINS

14-04 🅥

BD RASPAIL

MAISON DU FONTAINIER

AV. DENFERT-ROCHEREAU

14-111 🅥

RUE DE LA SANTÉ

FONDATION CARTIER

14-33 🅥

PLACE DENFERT ROCHEREAU

OBSERVATOIRE DE PARIS

RUE DE LA TOMBE-ISSOIRE

14-103 🅥

DENFERT ROCHEREAU Ⓜ

BD ARAGO

CATACOMBES

13-02 🅥

14-36 🅥

⑤

14-06 🅥

CATACOMBES

14-05 🅥

AV. RENÉ COTY

ST-JACQUES Ⓜ

BD SAINT-JACQUES

RUE DE LA GLACIÈRE

14-32 🅥

14-08 🅥

MOUTON DUVERNET Ⓜ

AV. DU GÉNÉRAL LECLERC

14-125 🅥

14-07 🅥

GLACIÈRE Ⓜ

BD AU

14-09 🅥

13-107 🅥

05-35

QUAI D'AU

BD DE L'HÔPITAL

10-33

13-14

05-15

CENSIER
DAUBENTON

05-34

05-105

13-13

ST-MARCEL

05-26

BD SAINT-MARCEL

13-06

13-103

05-27

GOBELINS

AV. DES GOBELINS

CAMPO
FORMIO

BD ARAGO

13-07

MANUFACTURE
DES GOBELINS

13-11

13-18

RUE JEANNE D'ARC

CHEVALERET

13-05

MOBILIER
NATIONAL

BD DE L'HÔPITAL

BD VINCENT-AURIOL

RUE PASCAL

AV. DES GOBELINS

SQUARE LE-GALL

13-08

PLACE
D'ITALIE

NATIONALE

13-10

13-17

13-43

13-101

3

13-09

PLACE
D'ITALIE

4

CORVISART

13-106

RUE DU CHÂTEAU-DES-RENTIERS

RUE BOBILLOT

AV. D'IVRY

QUARTIER
CHINOIS

A BUTTE-
UX-CAILLES

13-23

13-29

AV. D'ITALI

AV. DE CHOISY

13-34

13-22

13-122

OLYMPIADES

13-36

· Place d'Italie
· Les Olympiades – Chinatown
· Les Gobelins
· Mobilier National
· Les Frigos
· Îlot de la Reine-Blanche
· Square René-Le-Gall

13-35

|O| · Pho 14
· Lao Lane Xang
· Le Bambou
· Mageride

STAGE
3

13-39

· Tang Frères

LES DOCKS

13-20

POPB

BERCY
Ⓜ
12-25

12-105

12-108

QUAI DE LA RAPEE

BD DE BERCY

-FRANCE

12-26

CINEMATHEQUE
FRANÇAISE

RUE DE BERCY

PARC
DE BERCY

QUAI DE
LA GARE
Ⓜ
13-19

PASSERELLE
S.-DE-BEAUVOIR

13-123

12-31

COUR
ST ÉMILION
Ⓜ

MUSÉE DES
ARTS FORAINS

12-33

12-110

BIBLIOTHEQUE
NATIONALE DE FRANCE

QUAI FRANÇOIS MAURIAC

12-34

QUAI DE BERCY

DU CHEVALERET

13-15

13-51

LES FRIGOS

AV. DE FRANCE

BIBLIOTHÈQUE
FRANÇOIS
MITTERRAND
Ⓜ
13-53

13-54

13-16

BÉTONSALON

DE PATAY

13-45

13-55
Ⓜ

13-50

in a glass-and-steel building. The outside staircase is quite impressive, but best avoided if you suffer from a fear of heights!

🆅 No. 12-33 (opposite 28 Rue François-Truffaut, 12ᵉ).

Musée des Arts Forains

The magical Fairground Arts Museum is open to the public only by appointment and sometimes during the Christmas holidays. Its creator, Jean-Paul Favand, has collected thousands of beautifully preserved, rare artifacts: old fairground stalls, carousels, funfair attractions, toys, automata, curiosities, costumes, and scenery. When you walk into this museum, you're struck by the atmosphere of a whole other world. You'll want to touch and try everything – and you're allowed to! The merry-go-rounds still do go round, the little horses creaking slightly, and the paper lanterns and baroque chandeliers bathe the attractions in an unreal light.

53 Av. des Terroirs-de-France, 12ᵉ. 01 43 40 16 22. www.arts-forains.com – Check for opening times.
🆅 No. 12-110 (57-61 Rue des Pirogues-de-Bercy, 12ᵉ).

Taking a Break

BERCY VILLAGE
This unusual place seeped in history was the first retail and leisure complex in France. Its many shops offer you all you need to rethink your wardrobe, get a beauty make-over, satisfy your gourmet desires, and find the perfect present. Discover the unconventional elegance of Agnès b. and her line of clothing and accessories that allows everyone the freedom to express their own personality. Decorate your nest with the lovely selection of quality items on sale at Côté Maison and La Chaise Longue. During the summertime, Bercy Village invites music lovers from around the world onto its terrace for free concerts. Awesome!
🆅 No. 12-110 (57-61 Rue des Pirogues-de-Bercy, 12ᵉ).

FACTORY & CO
In Bercy, Factory & Co will be a pleasant surprise for both your palate and your wallet. Considered by some to be one of the best fast-food restaurants in the capital, it specializes in the famous bun. The buns are kneaded, shaped, and baked by bakers on the same day and filled with delicious, fresh ingredients, such as spicy tuna caviar, crispy bacon, smoked salmon and cream cheese, pastrami, and marinated chicken.
🍴 23 Cour Saint-Émilion, 12ᵉ. 01 43 07 47 01. www.factory-co.com – Open daily, noon–11pm.
🆅 No. 12-33 (28 Rue François-Truffaut, 12ᵉ).

CONCRÈTE
What if partying while watching the sun rise is the future of Parisian nights out? Concrète has become the indispensable meeting place of all the capital's clubbers. Head to the Quai de la Râpée for a unique Sunday that's every bit as good as a Berlin after-party. It's ten o'clock in the morning, people are crowding in, and sunglasses are obligatory on this gigantic barge that's been converted into a dance floor. Despite the odd setting, the hip population of Paris comes here especially to dance to the DJ's blazing beats, which can go on for hours. Concrète has brought in the heavy artillery with international names behind the decks. So now you see why Sunday mornings could be the future of Parisian Saturday nights out.
🚤 69 Port de la Râpée, 12ᵉ. www.concreteparis.fr – Open Sun, 7am–2pm.
🆅 No. 12-105 (153 Rue de Bercy, 12ᵉ).

BOCO
At Boco, Vincent and Simon have decided to bottle Anne-Sophie Pic, or rather put her tomato and galanga chutney in a jar. They've done the same, too, with Christophe Michalak of Plaza Athénée and his creamy mango and passionfruit cheesecake. So now you can eat these dishes either in their bistro or at your desk.
🍴 45 Cour Saint-Émilion, 12ᵉ. 01 46 28 96 60. www.bocobio.com – Open daily, 11am–10pm.
🆅 No. 12-33 (28 Rue François-Truffaut, 12ᵉ).

LE 51

Le 51 has one of the finest terraces in Paris. Open all year round, it looks over the park and offers you the chance to dine by moonlight, or to spend a lazy afternoon reclining on a sunlounger. The chefs propose a menu of dishes created with fresh, local, and seasonal produce.

📷 51 Rue de Bercy, 12ᵉ. 01 58 51 10 91.
www.restaurant51.com
Open Mon, 10am–6pm; Wed–Sun, 10am–11pm.
🚲 No. 12-26 (61 Rue de Bercy, 12ᵉ).

ERIC KAYSER

From sandwiches to *petits fours*, *croissants au beurre* to seasonal fruit tarts, everyone will find something to their taste here. This is also one of the best bakeries in Paris with rustic bread prepared with yeast and a multitude of flavours.
A pleasure to be enjoyed at any time of day!

🥖 41 Cour Saint-Émilion, 12ᵉ. 01 43 46 08 89.
www.maison-kayser.com – Open daily, 7am–11pm.
🚲 No. 12-33 (28 Rue François-Truffaut, 12ᵉ).

L'AUBERGE AVEYRONNAISE

In a neo-rustic and slightly Medieval setting, L'Auberge Aveyronnaise serves a fine selection of produce, including trout rillettes from Laguiole or a charcuterie platter to start with. Opt next for the *saucisse-aligot*, and finish your meal with the *millefeuille à l'ancienne*… This is cuisine that's in harmony with the tradition of Rouergue!

📷 40 Rue Gabriel-Lamé, 12ᵉ. 01 43 40 12 24.
www.auberge-aveyronnaise.fr
Open daily, noon–2:30pm and 7–11pm.
🚲 No. 12-31 (49 Rue Gabriel-Lamé, 12ᵉ).

ARTEUM

This concept store offers a selection of products and services related to the world of contemporary art, photography, and design. If you're not looking to acquire anything major yourself, there's also fun merchandise related to artists like Keith Haring, Basquiat, and Andy Warhol.

🛍 11 Cour Saint-Émilion, 12ᵉ. 01 55 78 99 06.
www.arteum.com – Open daily, 11am–9pm.
🚲 No. 12-33 (28 Rue François-Truffaut, 12ᵉ).

Calendar of Events

Exhibitions at the Cinémathèque de Paris
Scan this flashcode or visit
http://blog.velib.paris.fr/en/?s=cinemathequeparisEN

Cité de la Mode et du Design

② THE SEINE TODAY

✲ A Word From Vélib' ·····················

You have arrived on the Left Bank, and in one of the most modern and cosmopolitan areas in Paris. Cycle up Boulevard Vincent-Auriol. This is a quick and easy stage of your route: just keep going straight on, following the metro line overhead. The cycle path will take you to Place d'Italie, with the bonus of a nice slope to pedal up!

Passerelle Simone-de-Beauvoir

Have a look at this bridge, which is remarkable both technologically and aesthetically. Reserved for pedestrians and cyclists, the 37th bridge in Paris, opened in 2006, links the Parc de Bercy to the esplanade of the Bibliothèque François-Mitterrand. Because of its "lenticular" structure, you can also access the lower parts of the quayside.

🆅 No. 13-123 (53 Quai François-Mauriac, 13ᵉ).

Les Docks - Cité de la Mode et du Design

It's impossible to miss this glass-and-steel building on the Quai d'Austerlitz: it's in the shape of a lizard and painted bright green! It's difficult to imagine that this audacious contemporary (2008) edifice, the work of architects Jakob and MacFarlane, is actually a conversion of Paris's old general stores, a reinforced concrete structure dating back to 1907. Here you will find: "extramural" exhibitions organized by the Musée Galliera, the Institut Français de la Mode, galleries, bookshops, trendy boutiques, and nightlife (and daytime) hot spots.

34 Quai d'Austerlitz, 13ᵉ. 01 76 77 25 30.
🆅 No. 13-20 (15 Rue Paul-Klee, 13ᵉ).

The Left Bank of the 13th Arrondissement

A large-scale urban redevelopment program began in this neighbourhood in the 1990s with the building of the Bibliothèque François-Mitterrand (François-Mitterrand Library). It was continued with hundreds of thousands of square metres of residential buildings, offices, shops, cultural centres, and neighbourhood amenities, as well as an important university centre (Paris VII and "Langues O") in the old building of the Grands

Moulins de Paris (a converted industrial flourmill dating from the early 20th century). The long-barge-shaped MK2 Bibliothèque complex, which houses 14 cinemas, a bookstore, a specialist shop, and a café, has become an asset and a source of pride to the neighbourhood. So, too, have the Jardins des Abbé Pierre-Grands Moulins, an envi-ronmetally sustainable green space for relaxation that is enjoyed by the area's students and residents.

Bétonsalon

Centre for Art and Research, Bétonsalon is based at the Université Paris-VII, on the ground floor of the former flour market of the Grands Moulins de Paris. It seeks to establish "a space for reflection and debate between the arts and university research", gathering together artists, philosophers, scientists, sociologists, architects, playwrights, and choreographers to develop a variety of projects, including temporary exhibitions, workshops, conferences, publications, area tours, performances, etc.

9 Esplanade Pierre-Vidal-Naquet, 13ᵉ
(Ground floor of the Halle aux farines).
01 45 84 17 56. Open Tue–Sat, 11am–7pm (closed Aug).
🆅 No. 13-50 (23 Quai Panhard-et-Levassor, 13ᵉ).

Bibliothèque Nationale de France

The four glass towers (80 m/262 ft tall) look like open books: they belong to the very large library designed by D. Perrault and opened in 1994. This is the main site of the *Bibliothèque Nationale de France*. The *tour des lois* (law tower), *tour des lettres* (literature tower), *tour des nombres* (numbers tower) and *tour des temps* (history tower) hold more than ten million works, which are protected from sunlight by mobile wooden shutters. The garden below is sandwiched between two levels of lecture theatres. Sadly, it is not open to the public, but you can, like the students, sit in the sunshine on the esplanade steps and read.

Quai François-Mauriac, Paris 13ᵉ. www.bnf.fr
🆅 No. 13-123 (53 Quai François-Mauriac, 13ᵉ)
and No. 13-51 (9 Quai François-Mauriac, 13ᵉ).

M.O.B.

Fancy a burger, hot dog, or slice of cheesecake? All that's possible here, but it's all vegetarian! This Paris outlet of the New York restaurant that was hailed by the Daily News as the "best vegetarian restaurant" in the Big Apple, is located on the docks with a beautiful view over the Seine.

◉ 32 Quai d'Austerlitz, 13ᵉ.

Ⓥ No. 13-20 (15 Rue Paul-Klee, 13ᵉ).

WANDERLUST

This is the place that rocks the Left Bank: with its 1600 m² (17,200 ft²) terrace, the largest in Paris; a 200 m² (2150 ft²) club; a restaurant that seats 100; DJ sets that would make the biggest clubs on the French Riviera jealous; an open-air cinema; and a relaxation area with sun loungers, yoga classes, and a brunch bar on weekends, Wanderlust is a real breath of fresh air for the Paris nightlife scene. Who said that Paris was a city that sleeps?

🚠 32 Quai d'Austerlitz, 13ᵉ.

www.wanderlustparis.com – Open Thu–Sat, 8pm–6am.

Ⓥ No. 13-20 (15 Rue Paul-Klee, 13ᵉ).

JOSÉPHINE-BAKER POOL

You will love this swimming pool because it gives you the impression you're swimming in the Seine! The capital's 37th swimming pool benefits from the latest technology in terms of environmental protection. Water management is ecological: water is taken from the Seine to be made potable, then used for all the pool's requirements, and after being treated, returned to the river. The solarium will be the envy of those who've driven for ten hours to get a tan at the beach. And in the summer, the swimming pool is uncovered, to the delight of Parisians.

Quai de la Gare, 13ᵉ.

Ⓥ No. 13-123 (53 Quai François-Mauriac, 13ᵉ).

NÜBA

On the initiative of the team at Le Baron, Nüba has opened up on the roof of the Cité de la Mode et du Design. It's a festive spot that opens its garden when it's not raining. You can have a drink here, or enjoy a burger and real Belgian chips in a setting that'll make you feel you're on fries. Also watch a little video of the nocturnal ascent of the chip stall on the upper terrace of the docks with, as a bonus, a view across Paris.

🚠 Cité de la mode et du design. 32 Quai d'Austerlitz, 13ᵉ.

Ⓥ No. 13-20 (15 Rue Paul-Klee, 13ᵉ).

COCO DE MER

Don't worry if you can't afford a plane ticket: Coco de Mer will transport you to the beaches of the Indian Ocean as though by magic. Surrounded by palm trees, with your table lit by candlelight, and your feet in the sand, you just need to taste the cocktails and you'll be there. All that's missing is the sound of the waves. The staff, from the Seychelles, will serve you traditional recipes and fish flown in directly from the islands. An exotic vacation for your palate is guaranteed!

◉ 34 Bd. Saint-Marcel, 5ᵉ. 01 47 07 06 64.

www.cocodemer.fr – Closed Mon lunch and Sun.

Ⓥ No. 13-06 (2 Rue Duméril, 13ᵉ).

Joséphine-Baker Pool

PETIT BAIN

Floating beside the Quai François-Mauriac, Petit Bain offers, on three levels, a restaurant seating 70, a 450-place music venue, and a planted terrace. In the evening, the barge hosts emerging artists and hybrid music: Vietnamese rock, Turkish tango, or African hip-hop – all genres are welcomed here.

🚇 7 Port de la Gare, 13ᵉ. 01 80 48 49 81.
www.petitbain.org – Open Wed–Sat, 7:30–11pm.
🚲 No. 13-51 (9 Quai François-Mauriac, 13ᵉ).

CHEZ LILI ET MARCEL

This place is spacious and delightfully retro, like something straight out of the beginning of the last century. Folding seats, boxes, metal panels … it's a delight for the eyes as well as the taste buds. The homemade fries, incredibly tender meat, and hearty portions at a cheap price have won it lots of fans.

🍽 1 Quai d'Austerlitz, 13ᵉ. 01 45 85 00 08.
Open Mon–Fri, 6am–11:30pm; Sat and Sun, 8am–11pm.
🚲 No. 903 (1 Quai François-Mauriac, 13ᵉ).

BATOFAR

Both a live-music venue and a club, Batofar is iconic due to its very distinctive architecture and its many annual events. Original and varied, it occupies a prime place in the Parisian music and cultural scene. Its terrace overlooking the Seine attracts a host of regulars in wintertime, as well as during the summer months.

🚇 Port de la Gare, 13ᵉ. 01 53 60 17 00. www.batofar.org
Open Tue–Sat, 7–11:30pm and lunchtimes Mon–Sat.
🚲 No. 13-51 (9 Quai François-Mauriac, 13ᵉ).

MOON ROOF

On the roof of Les Docks Cité de la Mode, Moon Roof provides tons of events to wake up the 13th arrondissement. Ideal for having a drink or smoking a hookah with friends, the terrace offers a breathtaking view of the Seine. The spacious lounge area provides an intimate and relaxing atmosphere in which to sip a cocktail.

🍸 34 Quai d'Austerlitz, 13ᵉ. 01 76 77 34 83.
Open daily, 5pm–2am.
www.moonroof.fr
🚲 No. 13-20 (15 Rue Paul-Klee, 13ᵉ).

LE PETIT GRUMEAU

In the mood for pancakes? Head for this little crêperie that makes crêpes and galettes to order and garnishes them according to your desire. All the classics are here, of course: ham, cheese, egg, mushrooms, tomato. Carnivores who can't pass up on meat will enjoy the galette with *steak haché*, egg, cheese, onions, tomatoes, and crème fraîche – a great alternative to a hamburger! And you can either eat them in the little restaurant here or take them away to enjoy elsewhere!

🍽 54 Bd. Saint-Marcel, 5ᵉ. 01 43 31 72 11.
Closed Mon lunchtime and Sun.
🚲 No. 13-06 (2 Rue Duméril, 13ᵉ).

125

Calendar of Events

Exhibitions and evenings at the Cité de la Mode
Scan this flashcode or visit http://blog.velib.paris.fr/en/?s=citemodedesignEN

126

🌟 **A Word From Vélib'** ••••••••••••••••••••
Stop here for a while to explore Paris's Chinatown or cross the Place d'Italie to join up with the Boulevard Auguste-Blanqui.

Place d'Italie

The Place d'Italie is a reminder that this was once the arrival point of the Roman road from Lyon. It was also the *barrière d'octroi* (toll-house), which, until the 19th century, separated Paris from Gentilly. Claude Ledoux had built two pavilions here (like at Denfert-Rochereau). They were burned during the Revolution and destroyed some years later. The most significant event in the square's history was the repression by Cavaignac, the Head of Government, of an uprising staged by workers. One of his men, General Bréa de Ludre, was murdered, after being struck and insulted; another, Mangin, was axed to death! The revolt was hardly contained… This "barrière d'Italie" is today a busy intersection between the east and south of Paris. In the centre of the square is a memorial to Maréchal Alphonse Juin, which was unveiled in 1983. On the forecourt of the city hall, Zadkine's *Le Retour du fils prodigue* accompanies newlyweds as they leave.

Ⓥ No. 13-10 (opposite 11 Pl. d'Italie, 13ᵉ).

Les Olympiades – Chinatown

In the 1970s, Italie 13, a real estate project led by architect Michel Holley, saw the emergence of Les Olympiades, eight towers and three low-rise buildings that are named after Olympic cities: Athens, Sapporo, Helsinki, Tokyo… They stand on a huge esplanade that covers the former Gare des Gobelins. Les Olympiades didn't have much success until the arrival of refugees from Vietnam, Laos, and Cambodia, who were happy to find cheap housing here. In this way a major Asian community became established around the towers, and later in what would become known as the "Choisy triangle", with restaurants and shops quickly opening up. Smell the fragrances wafting from the Tang Frères supermarket, frequented by locals and lovers of Asian cuisine, and enjoy Peking roast duck at one of the area's many good

Chinese restaurants. If you get the chance, don't miss the Chinese New Year celebrations with their incredible costume parades.

44 Av. d'Ivry, 13ᵉ.
Ⓥ No. 13-39 (2 Rue de la Pointe-d'Ivry, 13ᵉ) and No. 13-35 (116 Av. de Choisy, 13ᵉ).

Les Gobelins

In the early 17th century, Colbert, Minister of Finances for King Henri IV, bought workshops on the Faubourg Saint-Marceau (now Saint-Marcel) from the Gobelin family, who had made their fortune as dyers. He converted them into a "factory" to produce tapestries and other decorative objects to adorn the royal palaces and to offer as gifts to foreign guests. The magnificent creations of Les Gobelins soon acquired an international reputation. Until the Revolution became established, the tapestries tended to depict religious subjects or allegories of the deeds of the sovereign of the time. Today, the cartoons (designs created before weaving) are based on works by contemporary artists, such as Jean Arp, Fernand Léger, Alexander Calder, and Sonia Delaunay. If you like the designs, you can buy reproductions on Les Gobelins website: *www.gobelins.fr*!

Mobilier National

It is here that furniture and other items that adorn the official palaces, such as the Élysée, ministries, and embassies, are stored while they are repaired,

Chinatown

in transit, or simply in stock, waiting to find a taker. Unfortunately for the curious, the site is not open to the public. However, you can view the furniture and interesting objects in temporary exhibitions held at the Galerie des Gobelins.

42 Av. des Gobelins, 13ᵉ. 01 44 08 52 00.
www.mobiliernational.culture.gouv.fr
Temporary exhibtions: Tue–Sun, 11am–6pm.
For guided tours, check on arrival.
Free admission last Sun of the month.
Ⓥ No. 13-007 (42 Rue Le-Brun, 13ᵉ).

Les Frigos

Trains used to pull into these warehouses, which date from 1921, to deposit perishable goods in giant refrigerators. They were abandoned in 1969 when the covered markets moved out of the centre of Paris to set up at Rungis. The industrial buildings were then taken over by artists in a semi-squat set-up, but with the blessing of SNCF, who owned the warehouses! No. 91 Quai de la Gare, nicknamed "Les Frigos" (the fridges), became a centre for contemporary art, housing a hundred or so artists and artisans, who are now officially installed here. The site is now owned by the City of Paris and remains a dynamically creative place. You can visit the workshops during open studio days, as well as at exhibitions held at the Galerie L'Aiguillage.

19 Rue des Frigos, 13ᵉ. www.les-frigos.com
Ⓥ No. 13-16 (9 Rue Primo-Levi, 13ᵉ).

Îlot de la Reine-Blanche

It is said that early in 1393, to celebrate the marriage of a lady-in-waiting to the queen, King Charles VI organized a huge party at the Hôtel de la Reine-Blanche. But there was a fire, which killed four of the king's best friends. The king himself only narrowly escaped death, and the tragedy of the "Ball of the Burning Men" precipitated his descent into madness. The manor was destroyed, leaving in its place a street of the same name. Then, in the 17th century, the Gobelin family built their homes and other industrial buildings on the site. These have recently been restored as private apartments, using documents of the time to recreate the original layout of courtyards and buildings.

17 Rue des Gobelins, 13ᵉ.
Ⓥ No. 13-05 (2 Rue des Cordelières, 13ᵉ).

Square René-Le-Gall

In the 17th century, workers in factories, dyers, and tanneries came to enjoy themselves at the bars and *guinguettes* of the Île aux Singes, a small island located on the Bièvre, a river that now runs underground, which used to flow through Paris's 5th and 13th arrondissements before joining the Seine. In 1938, a large neo-Classical-style garden was built on this site, which today is named after a member of the Resistance who was killed by the Germans in 1942: René Le Gall. It's a perfect place for a picnic in the lovely rose garden, under the shade of an Indian chestnut planted in 1894, or for a walk along the tranquil paths. Here you will see a curious obelisk, typical of the 1930s, and a charming artificial stream, which evokes the passage of the Bièvre.

Entrances on Pl. de la Bergère-d'Ivry, Rue Croulebarbe, Rue Berbier-du-Mets, Rue Émile-Deslandres and Rue des Cordelières.
Ⓥ No. 13-07 (42 Rue Le-Brun, 13ᵉ)
and No. 13-101 (67-69 Rue Croulebarbe, 13ᵉ).

127

TANG FRÈRES
Welcome to the capital's most picturesque supermarket! The whole of the neighbourhood's Asian community comes to this undecorated and badly arranged hangar-like space to stock up on fruit, packet soups, soy milk, dried bananas, frozen wontons, jelly sweets, and Tsingtao or Singha beer. The Mandarin packagings will certainly leave you speechless, but the prices are low, so why not try the strange spicy-sauce-flavoured chips, for example?

489 Av. d'Ivry, 13ᵉ. 01 45 70 80 00.
Open Tue–Sat, 9am–8pm; Sun, 9am–1pm.
No. 13-39 (2 Rue de la Pointe-d'Ivry, 13ᵉ).

PHO 14
Feeling a bit hungry? You won't be blown away by the decor or the atmosphere here: it's a simple fast-food restaurant, but the soups will certainly tickle your tastebuds. The house specialties? The chicken and beef soups, the pork or chicken nems, the wontons, and the rice pancakes. Come during the week and get here early, as this restaurant is always packed!

114 Av. de Choisy, 13ᵉ.
01 45 83 61 15. Open daily, 9am–11pm.
No. 13-35 (116 Av. de Choisy, 13ᵉ).

LAO LANE XANG
The biggest assets of the Asian menu offered here are the excellent-quality Laotian and Thai specialties. It's a popular and affordable place in Chinatown and the cuisine is good and tasty. Tom yum soup, chicken with cashew nuts … it's hardly surprising that the locals love this restaurant!

102 Av. d'Ivry, 13ᵉ. 01 58 89 00 00.
Open daily, noon–3pm and 7–11pm.
No. 13-35 (116 Av. de Choisy, 13ᵉ).

LE BAMBOU
The main theme here? Bamboo, obviously! This Vietnamese restaurant is renowned in the area for the exotic change of scene it provides. An excellent menu of traditional dishes awaits you: papaya salad, crab and vermicelli soup, grilled meats, *bun bo*… Expect to eat here elbow-to-elbow with your fellow diners in typical local-restaurant style.

70 Rue Baudricourt, 13ᵉ. 01 45 70 91 75.
Open Tue–Sun, 11:30am–3:30pm and 6:30–10:30pm.
No. 13-37 (76 Av. d'Ivry, 13ᵉ).

MARGERIDE
This typically Parisian bistro run by Olivier Mialane specializes in traditional French dishes. On the menu you'll find *truffade*, *tripoux*, and charcuterie platters. Those with hearty appetites will be pleased with the generous portions, and carnivores will enjoy the good-quality meat. And the chef will serve you at any time of day!

1 Bd. Auguste-Blanqui, 13ᵉ. 01 45 80 95 68.
No. 13-09 (46 Bd. Auguste-Blanqui, 13ᵉ).

Calendar of Events
Chinese-community events
Scan this flashcode or visit http://blog.velib.paris.fr/en/?s=evenementchinoisEN

4 BUTTE-AUX-CAILLES

⭐ A Word From Vélib'

The Butte-aux-Cailles is situated on your left just at the point where the Boulevard Auguste-Blanqui bears to the right. If you're feeling athletic, you can cycle up the hill on your Vélib', but if you prefer, you can park it at the foot of the butte and climb up on foot. If you're pushed for time, simply continue on your way without stopping.

Butte-aux-Cailles

Pierre Caille gave his name to the 64 m (210 ft) hill planted with vines overlooking the Bièvre that he bought in 1543. The land was not annexed to Paris until 1860. It was an impoverished area, inhabited mostly by poor families of labourers, artisans, and merchants. Windmills (*moulins*) dominated the hill, hence the names of some of the streets here: "Moulin-des-Prés", "Moulinet". Today the area, which was beautifully renovated in the 1990s, has retained its village feel, because the presence of underground quarries prohibits the construction of heavy buildings. Stroll along the old Passages Boiton and Barrault, and around the picturesque "villas" of Petite Alsace and Petite Russie, and enjoy the many cafés and restaurants.

Petite Alsace and Petite Russie

Cycle to the Villa Daviel, a small cul-de-sac lined with workers' houses dating from the mid-1920s and made from cheap materials: brick and burstone. Breathe in deeply… There's a sweet country air in this part of Paris, and among the intoxicating fragrances, you may even be able to discern those of banana and fig trees! Continue a little way along Rue Daviel and you will arrive at the so-called "Petite Alsace". Park your Vélib' and enter the first garden city to be built in Paris, in 1913. Admire the 40 pavilions, with their Alsatian-style half-timbering, in the middle of a courtyard surrounded by large trees. And now lift your gaze for a moment. Above the farthest pavilions stands a tall grey wall: this was a former Citroën taxi garage. On the roof you'll see a collection of little white houses. This has come to be known as "Petite Russie", because they were built at the beginning of the 20th century by the garage owner, as housing for his taxi drivers, all of whom were of Russian descent.

DES CRÊPES ET DES CAILLES

A tiny, unpretentious local crêperie that knows how to attract its customers. It cheerfully welcomes little groups of friends into an intimate, marine setting, offering them a menu of galettes, crêpes, and traditional cider. It is renowned for providing unbeatable value for money. In addition, this place makes an ideal starting point for a stroll around the picturesque 13th arrondissement.

🍽 13 Rue de la Butte-aux-Cailles, 13ᵉ. 01 45 81 68 69. Open Mon–Sat, noon–3pm and 7:30–10pm.
Ⓥ No. 13-22 (27 Rue de la Butte-aux-Cailles, 13ᵉ).

L'OISIVETHÉ

Escape from the hustle and bustle of the city in this haven of peace, which combines indulgences and knitting. Knitters and crocheters meet together here to enjoy lunch during the week, brunch at weekends, homemade cakes, the fine selection of teas, and the hand-dyed wools that are imported directly from the US and the UK.

🍵 1 Rue Jean-Marie-Jégo, 13ᵉ. 01 53 80 31 33. Open Tue–Thu, noon–7pm; Fri–Sun, noon–8pm.
Ⓥ No. 13-23 (30 Rue Bobillot, 13ᵉ).

SPUTNIK

Lovers of happy hour and online games will love this unusual bar. It's the perfect place to have a drink without breaking the bank (you can get a pint of Guiness for the price of a half until 8pm) in a rock-music ambience. Created by a group of friends, this bar is ideal for meeting people, especially on evenings when matches are shown on two screens.

🍷 14 Rue de la Butte-aux-Cailles, 13ᵉ. 01 45 65 19 82. www.sputnik.fr
Open daily, 11:30am–midnight (Sun from 4pm).
Ⓥ No. 13-23 (30 Rue Bobillot, 13ᵉ).

LES CAILLOUX

Run by true Italians, this restaurant is a genuine little Italian trattoria. The delicious menu proposes typically Florentine dishes made with fresh, tasty ingredients: antipasti, raviolis, calamari, linguine alla siciliana, tagliata… All in a relaxing setting.

🍽 58 Rue des Cinq-Diamants, 13ᵉ. 01 45 80 15 08. Open daily, noon–2:30pm and 7:30–11pm.
Ⓥ No. 13-22 (27 Rue de la Butte-aux-Cailles, 13ᵉ).

CHEZ GLADINES

This famous restaurant will take you on a journey to the Pays Basque for a very low price. Known for its wide range of salads served in huge salad bowls, Chez Gladines also serves traditional dishes of the South West of France, such as *chipirons à la biscaïana* (squid), *piperade* with braised ham, Basque tripe, and other Basque recipes…

🍽 30 Rue des Cinq-Diamants, 13ᵉ. 01 45 80 70 10. www.gladines-restaurant-paris.fr
Open daily, noon–3pm and 7pm–midnight (closed Sun eve).
Ⓥ No. 13-22 (27 Rue de la Butte-aux-Cailles, 13ᵉ).

LE VILLAGE DE LA BUTTE

This restaurant, which also serves as a bar and tobacconist, specializes in the cuisine of the Auvergne. Enjoy pâté, cured ham, saucisson, *croques* (toasted sandwiches), or eggs served on a bed of salad, all in a rustic setting with exposed beams. Simple and successful cooking that has attracted regulars.

🍽 23 Rue de la Butte-aux-Cailles, 13ᵉ. 01 45 80 36 82. Open Mon–Fri, 7am–1:30am; Sat, 8am–1:30am; Sun, 8am–midnight
Ⓥ No. 13-22 (27 Rue de la Butte-aux-Cailles, 13ᵉ).

LE MERLE MOQUEUR

A stone's throw from Parc Montsouris, Le Merle Moqueur welcomes you into a tropical and African setting where cocktails rule. The atmosphere here is warm, lively, and relaxed with background music of a mixture of styles. It's simple: you can drink your rum here for an unbeatable price, and in friendly place to boot.

🍷 11 Rue de la Butte-aux-Cailles, 13ᵉ. 01 45 65 12 43. Open daily, 5pm–2am.
Ⓥ No. 13-22 (27 Rue de la Butte-aux-Cailles, 13ᵉ).

LA FOLIE EN TÊTE

La Folie en Tête, which has become an iconic address of the Butte-aux-Cailles, stands out from the area's trendy bars. The decor is eclectic and the price of drinks easily affordable. All ages are welcome and the musical ambience ranges from world to rock and jazz.

🍷 33 Rue de la Butte-aux-Cailles, 13ᵉ. 01 45 80 65 99. Open Mon–Sat, 5pm–2am; Sun, 6pm–midnight.
Ⓥ No. 13-22 (27 Rue de la Butte-aux-Cailles, 13ᵉ).

STAGE 5 — DENFERT-ROCHEREAU

❋ A Word From Vélib'

This last stage won't be the most restful of the route: one of the most beautiful false flats in Paris awaits you on the cycle path along the Boulevards Auguste-Blanqui and Saint-Jacques to Place Denfert-Rochereau. There you'll finally be able to take a breather, or head off underground to explore the Catacombs.

The Catacombs

Yes! Under Place Denfert-Rochereau, there are bones and skulls, and you can go and see them! In the 18th century, the problem of the unsanitary conditions of cemeteries and other burials sites in Paris became unbearable and it was decided to move the bodies to a place that was easier to maintain. The old underground quarry of Tombe-Issoire welcomed into its galleries 20 m (66 ft) underground the bones of more than six million Parisians, famous in France's history or unknown, that were moved here between 1786 and 1814. As everything was anonymous and secular, the bones were lined up and the skulls piled up more or less artistically to show a bit of decorum. There are also some Baroque funerary monuments and commemorative plaques. To explore this macabre and fascinating place, wear something warm (the average temperature underground is 14°C/57°F); and put out good shoes to climb the 130 steps down into the galleries.

1 Av. du Colonel-Henri-Rol-Tanguy, 14e. 01 43 22 47 63. www.catacombes-de-paris.fr – Open Tue–Sun, 10am–5pm. ⓥ No. 14-05 (2 Av. René-Coty, 14e).

Carrière des Capucins

If you really can't face lining up to visit the Catacombs, and skeletons bore you, you could visit another part of the area's underground quarries that is much less well know but equally interesting. Over many years, an association of enthusiasts has been restoring the old Capucins quarries, stones from which were used, during the 15th and 16th centuries, for the building of the chapel of the Capucin monastery and in the construction of Notre-Dame cathedral. The guided tour, which takes two hours and is led by volunteers, starts with the descent of around 100 steps. The galleries, none of which is wider than the width of a man with a wheelbarrow, are bathed in the strange light of sodium lamps (used for ecological reasons) and give the visit an unreal aura. The dank passageways lead to the very beautiful Fontaine des Capucins. You'll need the same clothing and footwear as for the catacombs!

27 Rue du Faubourg-Saint-Jacques, 14e. It's worth a visit: E-mail: Jlhr-faure@wanadoo.fr, or write to the Association SEADACC, c/o Hôpital Cochin. ⓥ No. 14-04 (111 Bd. de Port-Royal, 14e).

131

Calendar of Events

Spend Halloween in Paris Scan this flashcode or visit http://blog.velib.paris.fr/en/?s=halloweenparisEN

The Catacombs

The observatory

Paris Observatory

This is the oldest astonomical observatory still in operation. In 1667, the Paris Meridian was traced on the site just before the construction of the building, which was commissioned by the members of Louis XIV's Academy of Sciences. Over the years, the observatory has been directed by leading scientists and has seen some important discoveries and achievements.

In the late 19th century, Arago made the first daguerreotype of the Sun here; Le Verrier founded the first weather stations; and Admiral Mouchez conceived, along with 180 other observatories throughout the world, the first map of the sky. It was here, too, that the first speaking clock was created, in 1933. Today, the observatory remains the principal French centre for research and university education in astronomy, with other establishments at Meudon and Nancy.

61 Av. de l'Observatoire, 14ᵉ. 01 40 51 22 21.
www.obspm.fr
Ⓥ No. 14-111 (18 Rue Cassini, 14ᵉ).

Maison du Fontainier

This astonishing 17th-century house is a *regard*, one of the openings allowing access to the Rungis (or Medicis) aquaduct. The *fontainier* was the Quartermaster General of the Water and Fountains of King Henri IV, who lived in the upper part of the house. In the basement, he managed the distribution of the water between the Palais du Luxembourg, the new residence of Queen Marie de Medicis, the fountains of Paris, and the area's many religious communities. You can visit the splendid vaulted rooms, the canalization systems, and the basin where the water emerges.

42 Av. de l'Observatoire, 14ᵉ. 01 48 87 74 31.
www.paris-historique.org
Ⓥ No. 14-111 (18 Rue Cassini, 14ᵉ).

Fondation Cartier

See route 6, p. 99.

261 Bd. Raspail, 14ᵉ. 01 42 18 56 50.
www. fondation.cartier.com
Ⓥ No. 14-03 (2 Rue Victor-Schœlcher , 14ᵉ).

Val-de-Grâce

In 1638, Anne of Austria gave birth to a son after more than 20 years of marriage: the future King Louis XIV. In gratitude for having been able to provide an heir to the throne of France, she wished to fulfil her vow to build a church dedicated to the Nativity in the Abbaye du Val-de-Grâce. Alas, her husband, Louis XIII, refused. It was not until he died, five years later, that she could envisage building her "magnificent temple". Since the Revolution, Val-de-Grâce has been a famous military hospital, where people from around the world come to receive treatment. The splendid Baroque church is worth a visit, and for those interested in medical objects, there's a museum of health services on the site of the abbey's former kitchen garden.

1 Pl. Alphonse-Laveran, 5ᵉ. 01 40 51 40 91.
www.valdegrace.org
Ⓥ No. 05-04 (272 Rue Saint-Jacques, 5ᵉ).

Calendar of Events
Exhibitions
at Fondation Cartier
Scan this flashcode or visit
http://blog.velib.paris.fr/
en/?s=fondationcartierEN

Taking a Break

RUE DAGUERRE
Why fill up your cart at the local supermarket when you could do your shopping on your Vélib', and buy good, fresh, organic produce for a bargain?! Rue Daguerre draws the crowds with its beautiful fruit and vegetables, its *appellations contrôlées* meats, and its inspired cheeses. But you could just wander around and enjoy soaking up the atmosphere of this market and the great smells of homegrown produce.
No. 14-36 (14 Rue Boulard, 14ᵉ).

CHAPLIN DENFERT
Three small cinema screens show a host of recent-release cartoons and films for children on Wednesdays and on weekends. You can even arrange to celebrate your birthday here and invite your friends. The cinema also offers popcorn and sweets and a workshop of your choice.
24 Pl. Denfert-Rochereau, 14ᵉ. 01 43 21 41 01.
www.cinemadenfert.fr
No. 14-05 (2 Av. René-Coty, 14ᵉ).

CAFÉ DU RENDEZ-VOUS
This café, which has been a family affair since 1979, was recently taken over by a thirtysome-thing couple who have decided to redo the decor to reflect their own young, modern style. They have, however, retained its Parisian bistro traditions and use seasonal, local produce.
2 Av. du Général-Leclerc, 14ᵉ. 01 43 21 34 05.
www.cafedurendezvous.com – Open daily, 7am–2am.
No. 14-05 (2 Av. René-Coty, 14ᵉ).

LES PIPELETTES
This is the story of two *pipelettes* (chatterboxes) who decided to quit office life to devote themselves instead to their passion: eating well. Always on the lookout for the latest culinary trends, they offer three different menu choices – or *dînettes*, as they call them – every day.
29 Rue Brezin, 14ᵉ. 09 81 29 27 32. Open Tue–Sat, 11am–7pm.
No. 14-08 (8 Rue Mouton-Duvernet, 14ᵉ).

LES PETITES SORCIÈRES
The former Michelin-starred chef of Pavillon Ledoyen brings a Nordic touch to the cuisine here. Simple, gourmet, and fresh, her reinvented bistro dishes will delight your palate without damaging your wallet!
12 Rue Liancourt, 14ᵉ. 01 43 21 95 68.
Open Tue–Sat, noon–2:30pm and 7–10:15pm.
No. 14-36 (14 Rue Boulard, 14ᵉ).

CHEZ BOGATO
This cake paradise will tickle the taste buds of those with a sweet tooth. Created by former art director Anaïs Olmer, these desserts are all out of the ordinary – a pound cake shaped and decorated to look like a safe, a chocolate cake shaped like a slipper – and there are some very original flavourings.
7 Rue Liancourt, 14ᵉ. 01 40 47 03 51.
www.chezbogato.fr – Open Tue–Sat, 10am–7pm.
No. 14-36 (14 Rue Boulard, 14ᵉ).

DISC'KING IV
Diehard film fans with limited means will love this temple of the disc. You can find some very good classics here, like little rare pearls, for as little as €2.90 a DVD. It's the perfect place not only for film-lovers but also for those who love music, as they have a very good selection of CDs at low prices, too.
15 Rue Daguerre, 14ᵉ. 01 43 22 53 55.
Open Mon–Sat, 10:30am–7:30pm.
No. 14-36 (14 Rue Boulard, 14ᵉ).

BULLES DE SALON
A bookstore for comic fans! You will find comics and graphic novels of all genres in this Canal BD outlet: Franco-Belgian classics, American comics, and mangas.
87 Rue Daguerre, 14ᵉ. 01 43 20 47 89.
www.bullesdesalon.com
Open Mon–Sat, 11am–8pm; Sun, 10am–2pm.
No. 14-103 (132 Av. du Maine, 14ᵉ).

LA CHOPE DAGUERRE
With its soft banquettes on the terrace, this bar attracts passersby on Rue Daguerre. The menu varies seasonally, offering fresh produce year round. Their vast selection of wines is also excellent, including the cheaper bottles!
17 rue Daguerre, 14ᵉ. 01 43 22 76 59.
Open Mon–Fri, 6am–11:30pm; Sat and Sun, 8am–11pm.
No. 14-05 (2 Av. René-Coty, 14ᵉ).

Bonus Paris Respire!

This guide has got you cycling on a few sections of the 12 cycle routes recommended by the City of Paris. But exploring Paris doesn't stop there! Continue your adventures on the 700 km (435 mi) of available routes and discover the "Paris Respire" zones! To make your Sunday outings, whether on Vélib' or on foot, even more enjoyable, think about taking advantage of this additional program.

....

"PARIS RESPIRE" – HOW DOES IT WORK?

Every Sunday and on public holidays, certain roads and areas in Paris are closed to motorized vehicles. "Paris Respire" thus gives pedestrians, cyclists, and rollerskaters free and exclusive access to roads usually used by motorists. This is your chance to walk, cycle, or rollerskate around Paris in complete safety, with friends, as a couple, or with the children!

AT LEAST 16 PLACES INCLUDED

The roads are clear in the Marais, Montmartre, Sentier, along the banks of the Seine, and in the four corners of the capital – not forgetting the Bois de Boulogne and the Bois de Vincennes, where you can rent bikes for children, too. Paris awaits you and invites you on an adventure in the open air. If you like cycling, this is the time to get around by Vélib'!

Depending on the area, "Paris Respire" may also be scheduled on Saturdays, and certain districts take part in the scheme during the summer months. You'll therefore be spoiled for choice!

For more details on the areas involved, check the map opposite, and to find out about the dates and times of "Paris Respire" scheme visit the Vélib' & Moi blog. You're sure to find a good idea for a Sunday bike ride or walk.

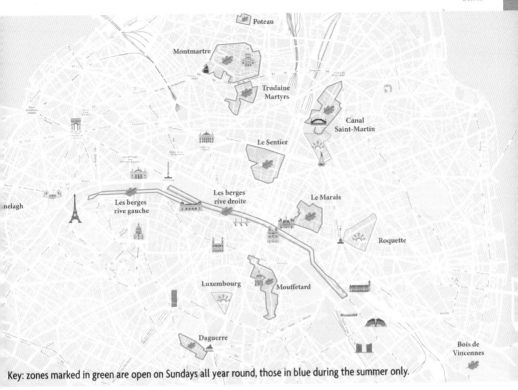

Poteau
Montmartre
Trudaine
Martyrs
Canal
Saint-Martin
Le Sentier
Les berges
rive gauche
Les berges
rive droite
Le Marais
nelagh
Roquette
Luxembourg
Mouffetard
Daguerre
Bois de
Vincennes

Key: zones marked in green are open on Sundays all year round, those in blue during the summer only.

Paris Respire

**or more information
on times and dates**
Scan this flashcode or visit
http://blog.velib.paris.fr/en/
?s=ParisRespireEN

Index

PLACES TO TAKE A BREAK

140

HOW TO SCAN A FLASHCODE WITH YOUR SMARTPHONE

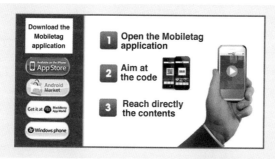

Download the Mobiletag application

Available on the iPhone — App Store
Android Market
Get it at BlackBerry App World
Windows phone

1 Open the Mobiletag application

2 Aim at the code

3 Reach directly the contents

LES GUIDES DU CHÊNE

DES GUIDES PAS COMME LES AUTRES

Paris by Bike with Vélib'

Seven cycle routes
for exploring Paris.

My Little Paris

My Little Paris, Kanako

The Paris only Parisians know!

My Little Lyon

My Little Lyon, Kanako

The Lyon of Lyonnaises!

Paris pour les hommes

Thierry Richard, Aseyn,
Juliette Ranck

The first city guide for men
who love Paris.

Paris de tous les plaisirs

Thierry Richard, Aseyn,
Juliette Ranck

A guide to the sensuous
side of Paris.

My Best Address Book

Chloé Bolloré, Laure Baubigeat

The guide to the most chic
and trendy places in Paris.

Paris fait son cinéma
Barbara Boespflug,
Béatrice Billon, P.-O. Signe

101 places that have inspired
the greatest films.

Guide de l'Italie à Paris
Valérie Vangreveninge,
Pierre-Olivier Signe

150 places to go
to find La Dolce Vita in Paris.

Guide du Japon à Paris
Minako Norimatsu,
Pierre-Olivier Signe

150 places to go
to find the best of Japan in Paris.

Véro trouve tout !
Véronique de Villèle,
Muriel Abadie

100 useful, novel, and cheap
places to go in Paris.

40 mystérieux
villages de France
Sylvie Steinebach

Legends, treasures, crypts,
relics: the guide to France's most
unusual villages.

Les chemins de Saint-
Jacques-de-Compostelle
Alexandra de Lassus,
Charlotte du Jour

The essential guide
for novice pilgrims.

Chien des villes
Brigitte Bulard-Cordeau

Walks, leisure, training,
grooming, style: the smart
guide for urban dogs.

Les mamans testent
Marie Perarnau, Chloé Perarnau,
Antoine Vanoverschelde

The survival kit for raising
and loving your children!

My Little Day
Gabriella Toscan du Plantier,
Dorothée Monestier, Iris De Moüy

Everything you need
to plan your child's birthday.

The publisher would like to thank the Mairie de Paris and all the whole Vélib' & Moi blog team for their responsiveness and enthusiastic support.

The Brand Marketing and Communication Department of the Marie de Paris would like to thank the JCDecaux Group, the Department of Roads and Transport, the Convention and Visitors Bureau of Paris, and the photographic service of the Mairie de Paris for their invaluable assistance.

Managing Editor: Juliette de Lavaur
Project Editor: Françoise Mathay, assisted by Marion Dellapina and Marie-Astrid Pourchet
Translation: Anne McDowall
Proofreading: Nina Holt
Editorial research: Aurélie Clair
Art direction: Sabine Houplain, assisted by Claire Mieyeville and Audrey Lorel
Design and layout: Gaëlle Junius
Production: Marion Lance
Co-editions and direct sales: Claire Le Cocguen (clecocguen@hachette-livre.fr)
Press relations: Hélène Maurice (hmaurice@hachette-livre.fr)
Colour reproduction: Les PAOistes

Mairie de Paris
Anne-Sylvie Schneider, Information and Communication Director
Gildas Robert, Brand Marketing and Communication Manager
Wilfried Hubert, Project Manager responsible for monitoring this work
Elisabeth Dubost, Licensing Agent for Vélib' - Arborescence

With the collaboration of Vélib' & moi – blog.velib.paris.fr – ©Vélib' - Mairie de Paris, 2013.
Text by: Gyl Cail, Beatriz Job, Anne-Sophie Mei, Muriel Nathan-Deiller, Aurélie Razat, Aurélie Rozier, Marion Seunevel, Rachel Thomas, Noélie Viallet.
Art Direction (maps and illustrations): Wilfried Hubert, Catherine Lacombe - Calac
Illustrations: « Mesdemoiselles » (Aurélie Castex and Claire Laude) – http://mesdemoiselles.fr
Maps: JCDecaux
Photo Credits: Photographs by the Office du Tourisme et Service Photographique de la Ville de Paris: H. Cardi: p. 114. H. Garat: p. 15, 24, 78 (d.), 84 (g. et d.), 92 (d.), 99 (d.), 126, 131 (g.). J.-B. Gurliat (d.): p. 42, 45 (g.), 50, 67 (d.), 90 (g.), 92 (g.), 116, 135 (g.). G. Guyon (g.): p. 30, 71. A.-L. Delhay: p. 66, 67 (g.). F. Le Dréau (d.): p. 42, 43 (g.), 64. D. Lesage: p. 20, 117. S. Magaud: p. 98. R. Mesnildrey: p. 26 (d.). H. Parrenne: p. 104 (g.). A. Paufert: p. 26 (g.). C. Pignol: p. 78 (d.). S. Robichon: p. 28 (g. et d.), 36 (g.), 45 (d.), 52, 58 (g.), 78 (g.), 82 (g.), 85 (d.), 90 (d.), 94, 104 (d.), 111 (g.), 124-125. A. Tézenas: p. 99. A. Thomes: p. 29, 40 (g.), 131 (d.). D. Vélasquez p. 58 (d.). M. Verhille (d.): p. 30, 61.

Original edition published in 2013 by Les Éditions du Chêne.
© Hachette Livre, Éditions du Chêne, 2013 – www.editionsduchene.fr

Édité par Les Éditions du Chêne (43, quai de Grenelle, 75905 Paris Cedex 15).

Printed by Estella Graficas
(CRTA Estella Tafalla km2, 31200 Estella Navarra, Spain)
Printed in June 2013 – Legal deposit: July 2013
ISBN 978-2-81230-851-2
32/3753/4-01